Jen Wilkin

# Better

## A Study of Hebrews

LifeWay Press® Nashville, Tennessee

Published by LifeWay Press® • © 2019 Jen Wilkin
Reprinted September 2020

## EDITORIAL TEAM
## ADULT MINISTRY PUBLISHING

Faith Whatley
*Director, Adult Ministry*

Michelle Hicks
*Manager, Adult Ministry*
*Short Term Bible Studies*

Elizabeth Hyndman
*Content Editor*

Sarah Doss
*Production Editor*

Lauren Ervin
*Graphic Designer*

Chelsea Waack
*Graphic Designer*

Micah Kandros Design
*Cover Designer*

ISBN: 978-1-5359-5411-2

Item: 005814378

Dewey Decimal Classification: 227.87
Subject Headings: BIBLE. N.T. HEBREWS—STUDY AND TEACHING/JESUS CHRIST

To order additional copies of this resource, order online at www.lifeway.com; write LifeWay Christian Resources Customer Service: One LifeWay Plaza, Nashville, TN 37234-0113; fax order to 615.251.5933; or call toll-free 1.800.458.2772.

Printed in the United States of America

Adult Ministry Publishing
LifeWay Resources
One LifeWay Plaza
Nashville, TN 37234

Author is represented by Wolgemuth & Associates.

# Contents

# About the Author

Jen Wilkin is an author and Bible teacher from Dallas, Texas. She has organized and led studies for women in home, church, and parachurch contexts. Her passion is to see others become articulate and committed followers of Christ, with a clear understanding of why they believe what they believe, grounded in the Word of God. Jen is the author of *Women of the Word: How to Study the Bible with Both Our Hearts and Our Minds*, *None Like Him: 10 Ways God Is Different From Us (and Why That's a Good Thing)*, *In His Image: 10 Ways God Calls Us to Reflect His Character*, *God of Creation* Bible study, *God of Covenant* Bible study, *Sermon on the Mount* Bible study, and *1 Peter: A Living Hope in Christ* Bible study. You can find her at JenWilkin.net.

# Foreword: How Should We Approach God's Word?

## OUR PURPOSE

The Bible study you are about to begin will teach you an important passage of the Bible in a way that will stay with you for years to come. It will challenge you to move beyond loving God with just your heart, to loving Him with your mind. It will focus on answering the question, "What does the Bible say about God?" It will aid you in the worthy task of God-discovery.

You see, the Bible is not a book about self-discovery; it is a book about God-discovery. The Bible is God's declared intent to make Himself known to us. In learning about the character of God in Scripture, we will experience self-discovery, but it must not be the object of our study. The object must be God Himself.

This focus changes the way we study. We look first for what a passage can teach us about the character of God, allowing self-discovery to be the by-product of God-discovery. This is a much better approach because there can be no true knowledge of self apart from knowledge of God. So when I read the account of Jonah, I see first that God is just and faithful to His Word—He is faithful to proclaim His message to Nineveh no matter what. I see second that I, by contrast (and much like Jonah), am unjust to my fellow man and unfaithful to God's Word. Thus, knowledge of God leads to true knowledge of self, which leads to repentance and transformation. So are confirmed Paul's words in Romans 12:2 that we are transformed by the renewing of our minds.

Most of us are good at loving God with our hearts. We are good at employing our emotions in our pursuit of God. But the God who commands us to love with the totality of our hearts, souls, and strength also commands us to love Him with all of our minds. Because He only commands what He also enables His children to do, it must be possible for us to love Him well with our minds or He would not command it. I know you will bring your emotions to your study of God's Word, and that is good and right. But it is your mind that I am jealous for. God intends for you to be a good student, renewing your mind and thus transforming your heart.

## OUR PROCESS

Being a good student entails following good study habits. When we sit down to read, most of us like to read through a particular passage and then find a way to apply it to our everyday lives. We may read through an entire book of the Bible over a period of time, or we may jump around from place to place. I want to suggest a different approach, one that may not always yield immediate application, comfort, or peace, but one that builds over time a cumulative understanding of the message of Scripture.

### READING IN CONTEXT AND REPETITIVELY

Imagine yourself receiving a letter in the mail. The envelope is handwritten, but you don't glance at the return address. Instead you tear open the envelope, flip to the second page, read two paragraphs near the bottom, and set the letter aside. Knowing that if someone bothered to send it to you, you should act on its contents in some way, you spend a few minutes trying to figure out how to respond to what the section you just read had to say. What are the odds you will be successful?

No one would read a letter this way. But this is precisely the way many of us read our Bibles. We skip past reading the "envelope"—Who wrote this? To whom is it written? When was it written? Where was it written?— and then try to determine the purpose of its contents from a portion of the whole. What if we took time to read the envelope? What if, after determining the context for its writing, we started at the beginning and read to the end? Wouldn't that make infinitely more sense?

In our study, we will take this approach to Scripture. We will begin by placing our text in its historical and cultural context. We will "read the envelope." Then we will read through the entire text multiple times, so that we can better determine what it wants to say to us. We will read repetitively so that we might move through three critical stages of understanding: comprehension, interpretation, and application.

## STAGE 1: COMPREHENSION

Remember the reading comprehension section on the SAT? Remember those long reading passages followed by questions to test your knowledge of what you had just read? The objective was to force you to read for detail. We are going to apply the same method to our study of God's Word. When we read for comprehension we ask ourselves, "What does it say?" This is hard work. A person who *comprehends* the account of the six days of creation can tell you specifically what happened on each day. This is the first step toward being able to interpret and apply the story of creation to our lives.

## STAGE 2: INTERPRETATION

While comprehension asks, "What does it say?," interpretation asks, "What does it mean?" Once we have read a passage enough times to know what it says, we are ready to look into its meaning. A person who *interprets* the creation story can tell you why God created in a particular order or way. She is able to imply things from the text beyond what it says.

## STAGE 3: APPLICATION

After doing the work to understand what the text says and what the text means, we are finally ready to ask, "How should it change me?" Here is where we draw on our God-centered perspective to ask three supporting questions:

- What does this passage teach me about God?
- How does this aspect of God's character change my view of self?
- What should I do in response?

A person who *applies* the creation story can tell us that because God creates in an orderly fashion, we, too, should live well-ordered lives. Knowledge of God gleaned through comprehension of the text and interpretation of its meaning can now be applied to my life in a way that challenges me to be different.

## SOME GUIDELINES

It is vital to the learning process that you allow yourself to move through the three stages of understanding on your own, without the aid of commentaries or study notes. The first several times you read a passage, you will probably be confused. In our study together, not all the homework questions will have answers that are immediately clear to you. This is actually a good thing. If you are unsure of an answer, give it your best shot. Allow yourself to feel lost, to dwell in the "I don't know." It will make the moment of discovery stick. We'll also expand our understanding in the small group discussion and teaching time.

Nobody likes to feel lost or confused, but it is an important step in the acquisition and retention of understanding. Because of this, I have a few guidelines to lay out for you as you go through this study:

1. **Avoid all commentaries** until *comprehension* and *interpretation* have been earnestly attempted on your own. In other words, wait to read commentaries until after you have done the homework, attended small-group time, and listened to the teaching. And then, consult commentaries you can trust. Ask a pastor or Bible teacher at your church for suggested authors. I used the following commentaries in creating this study: *Word Biblical Commentary: Hebrews 1–8 and Hebrews 9–13* by William L. Lane, *The New International Commentary on the New Testament: The Epistle to the Hebrews* by F. F. Bruce, and *The Pillar New Testament Commentary: The Letter to the Hebrews* by Peter O'Brien.

2.  For the purposes of this study, **get a Bible without study notes.** Come on, it's just too easy to look at them. You know I'm right.

3.  Though commentaries are initially off-limits, here are some **tools you should use:**

    - **Cross-references.** These are the Scripture references in the margin or at the bottom of the page in your Bible. They point you to other passages that deal with the same topic or theme.

    - **An English dictionary** to look up unfamiliar words. A good online dictionary is: http://www.merriam-webster.com/.

    - **Other translations of the Bible.** We will use the English Standard Version (ESV) as a starting point, but you can easily consult other versions online. I recommend the Christian Standard Bible (CSB), New International Version (NIV), New American Standard Version (NASB), or the New King James Version (NKJV). Reading more than one translation can expand your understanding of the meaning of a passage. Note: a paraphrase, such as The Message, can be useful but should be regarded as a commentary rather than a translation. They are best consulted after careful study of an actual translation.

    - **A printed copy of the text,** double-spaced, so you can mark repeated words, phrases, or ideas. On page 167 of your Bible study book you will find a printed copy of the Book of Hebrews. You will need it to complete your homework each week. You will also need a set of colored pens or pencils. We will be marking key words or phrases, as well as looking up some words in the dictionary.

## STORING UP TREASURE

Approaching God's Word with a God-centered perspective, with context, and with care takes effort and commitment. It is study for the long-term. Some days your study may not move you emotionally or speak to an immediate need. You may not be able to apply a passage at all. But what if ten years from now, in a dark night of the soul, that passage suddenly opens up to you because of the work you have done today? Wouldn't your long-term investment be worth it?

In Matthew 13 we see Jesus begin to teach in parables. He tells seven deceptively simple stories that leave His disciples struggling for understanding—dwelling in the "I don't know," if you will. After the last parable, He turns to them and asks, "Have you understood all these things?" (v. 51a). Despite their apparent confusion, they answer out of their earnest desire with, "Yes" (v. 51b). Jesus tells them that their newfound understanding makes them "like the owner of a house who brings out of his storeroom new treasures as well as old" (13:52, NIV).

A storeroom, as Jesus indicates, is a place for keeping valuables over a long period of time for use when needed. Faithful study of God's Word is a means for filling our spiritual storerooms with truth, so that in our hour of need we can bring forth both the old and the new as a source of rich provision. I pray that this study would be for you a source of much treasure and that you would labor well to obtain it.

Grace and peace,

Jen Wilkin

# How to Use This Study

This Bible study book is designed to be used in a specific way. The homework in the Bible study book will start you in the process of comprehension, interpretation, and application. However, it was designed to dovetail with small-group discussion time and the teaching sessions. You can use the Bible study book by itself, but you are likely to find yourself with some unresolved questions. The teaching sessions are intended to resolve most, if not all, of your unanswered questions from the homework and discussion time. With this in mind, consider using the materials as follows:

- If you are going through the study **on your own**, first work through the homework, and then watch or listen to the corresponding teaching for that week.

- If you are going through the study **in a group**, first do your homework, and then discuss the questions your group decides to cover. Then watch or listen to the teaching. Some groups watch or listen to the teaching before they meet, which can also work if that format fits best for everyone.

Note: For Week One, there is no homework. The study begins with an audio or video introduction. You will find a Viewer Guide on pages 14–15 that you can use as you watch or listen to the introductory material.

# How to Use the Leader Guide

At the end of each week's homework you will find a leader guide intended to help facilitate discussion in small groups. Each guide begins with an introductory question to help group members get to know each other and feel comfortable contributing their voices to the discussion. These questions may prove to be most helpful during the early weeks of the study, but as the group grows more familiar with one another, group leaders may decide to skip them to allow more time for the questions covering the lesson.

The remainder of the leader guide includes questions to help group members compare what they have learned from their homework on Days Two through Five. These questions are either pulled directly from the homework, or they summarize a concept or theme that the homework covered. Each two-part question covers content from a particular day of the homework, first asking group members to reflect and then asking them to apply. The reflection questions typically ask group members to report a finding or flesh out an interpretation. The application questions challenge them to move beyond intellectual understanding and to identify ways to live differently in light of what they have learned.

As a small group leader, you will want to review these questions before you meet with your group, thinking through your own answers, marking where they occur in the homework, and noting if there are any additional questions that you might want to reference to help the flow of the discussion. These questions are suggestions only, intended to help you cover as much ground as you can in a 45-minute discussion time. They should not be seen as requirements or limitations, but as guidelines to help you prepare your group for the teaching time by allowing them to process collectively what they have learned during their homework.

As a facilitator of discussion rather than a teacher, you are allowed and encouraged to be a colearner with your group members. This means you yourself may not always feel confident of your answer to a given question, and that is perfectly OK. Because we are studying for the long-term, we are allowed to leave some questions partially answered or unresolved, trusting for clarity at a later time. In most cases, the teaching time should address any lingering questions that are not resolved in the homework or the small-group discussion time.

# Week One:
## Hebrews Introduction

Who wrote the Book of Hebrews?

When was it written?

To whom was it written?

In what style was it written?

What is the central theme of the book?

# Week Two:

# Better than Angels

As we discussed in our introduction, repetitive reading of a book of the Bible helps you learn and retain its message. Hopefully, you have taken the opportunity to read through Hebrews already to get a high-level view of what we will be studying. Make an effort to continue to read the entire letter repetitively throughout the course of the study. Try to do so at least five times. As you read, think about what you learned in the introductory lesson. Think about the "archaeological questions" we answered about the letter. To read through Hebrews five times during the course of the study, try reading half of it each week. You could alternate reading chapters 1–6 on even weeks and chapters 7–13 on odd weeks.

Your weekly homework will focus in on a particular passage to see what it has to say and how it fits into the greater context of the letter as a whole. The homework is designed to help you take a closer look at what you are reading.

Let's get started.

**READ THIS WEEK'S PASSAGE: HEBREWS 1:1–2:18.**

1.  In 2–3 sentences, summarize the main ideas of the passage.

2.  According to this week's passage, who or what is Jesus Christ better than?

3.  Mark every occurrence of the word *angels* in this week's section of the text with a red A. How many occurrences did you find?

## NOW LOOK MORE CLOSELY AT HEBREWS 1:1-4.

4.  Based on these opening verses, what do you think the author's first concern was in writing his letter? What did he want to establish first and foremost in the minds of his hearers?

5.  In the space below, note everything you learn about Christ in these first four verses.

| WHO HE IS | WHERE HE IS | WHAT HE DOES/ HAS DONE |
| --- | --- | --- |
|  |  |  |

6.  What contrast did the author paint in 1:1-2? Pay attention to repeated words to help you answer.

Rewrite 1:1-2 below in your own words to capture what he was saying.

7.  What are some of the "many ways" God spoke to His people in the past (1:1)? Look up the following verses and note what you find.

    **Genesis 28:10-15**

    **Exodus 3:1-6**

    **Exodus 20:1-21**

    **Numbers 22:28,32**

    **2 Peter 1:21**

8.  What time period do you think the author was noting with the phrase "in these last days" (1:2a)?

9.  In 1:3-4 the author set up the contrast he would explore in the rest of chapters 1 and 2. Why might a contrast between Christ and angels have been necessary and helpful for his original hearers? Look up the following verses to help with your answer.

    **Colossians 2:18 • Revelation 22:8-9**

10. **APPLY:** Choose the description of Christ in 1:1-4 that is most surprising or impactful to you. Write it below.

How should the statement you chose above impact your perspective on how to live "in these last days" as one of Christ's followers?

**NOW LOOK AT HEBREWS 1:5-14.**

11. The author used seven different Old Testament passages to illustrate Christ's superiority to the angels (Ps. 2:7; 2 Sam. 7:14; Ps. 97:7; Ps. 104:4; Ps. 45:6-7; Ps. 102:25-27; Ps. 110:1). Based on what you know about his audience, why would this have been an effective strategy?

What does his effective use of these passages tell you about the author?

12. On the chart below, note the comparison between Christ and the angels in the verses indicated (some are stated explicitly and others are implied).

| | CHRIST | THE ANGELS |
|---|---|---|
| 1:5 | | |
| 1:5 | | |
| 1:7-9 | | |
| 1:10-12 | | |
| 1:13-14 | | |

13. **APPLY:** How can modern believers be guilty of giving misplaced attention—even worship—to the spiritual realm instead of to Christ? Why is it tempting to do so? Why is it dangerous?

**NOW LOOK AT HEBREWS 2:1-4.**

14. What important transitional word do you find at the beginning of 2:1?

Mark it in your copy of the text with **a purple capital T and underline.**

How does the message of 2:1 follow logically from what has just come before?

15. What is "the message declared by angels" referenced in 2:2? Look up the following verses to help with your answer.

Deuteronomy 33:2 • Acts 7:53 • Galatians 3:19

16. In 2:2 the author meant to stir the Old Testament memories of his Jewish Christian hearers. Based on your knowledge of the Old Testament, give two examples of times that disobedience received a just retribution.

How do these examples prove the reliability of the message the angels declared (God's law)?

17. What three reasons are given in 2:3-4 to establish the credibility of our salvation? Write them below. Next to each one, note what New Testament event or occurrence they likely describe.

    1.

    2.

    3.

18. **APPLY:** In what ways are modern believers prone to drift away or neglect the truth we know? What regular practices might help us "pay much closer attention to what we have heard" (2:1a)?

## NOW LOOK AT HEBREWS 2:5-18.

19. In 2:5-9 the author quoted and discussed Psalm 8:4-6, the section of the psalm describing humanity. Why do you think the author of Hebrews applied this psalm to Jesus in particular? What did he want us to understand? Compare Hebrews 2:9 to 1 Corinthians 15:22 to help with your answer.

20. Look at 2:10. In what way was Christ "made perfect through suffering"? Give your best answer. If you are unsure, start by thinking through what the phrase cannot mean, based on what you know is true about God.

21. In 2:10-18 mark every occurrence of *a familial term* (sons, brothers, children) with a blue underline. (Note: the term *sons* connotes *sons and daughters* and the term *brothers* connotes *brothers and sisters*. They can be properly read with no gendered connotation.)

    Why is it important for us to understand our salvation in family terms?

22. What reason is given for the death of Jesus in 2:14-15? Summarize these two verses below.

23. In 2:16 who does God help?

    Look up Romans 9:6-8 and Galatians 3:7 to clarify to whom this phrase is referring.

24. How does 2:16 contrast believers to angels? Are angels part of the family of God?

25. In 2:17-18 the author introduced the theme of Jesus as High Priest. He would develop this theme at length in later chapters. For now, look up the word *propitiation* in a dictionary or thesaurus, and write a definition for it below that best fits with the context of 2:17-18. Check the NIV Bible translation as well to see what word it uses.

    PROPITIATION: (Hint: look up *propitiate* and modify the definition to a noun form, or look up *propitiatory* in the thesaurus.)

26. APPLY: Reread 2:8. How much does Jesus, who calls you part of His family, control?

What area of your life feels most out of control? What news headline scares you the most? What sin feels unconquerable to you?

How does the truth in 2:7-9 speak peace to your greatest fears?

## WRAP-UP

What aspect of God's character has this week's passage of Hebrews shown you more clearly?

Fill in the following statement:

Knowing that God is _____ shows me that
I am _____.

What one step can you take this week to better live in light of this truth?

**INTRODUCTORY QUESTION:** What is your favorite book or movie about angels?

**1. OBSERVE:** (question 5, p. 19) Note everything you learn about Christ in the first four verses of Hebrews.

**APPLY:** (question 10, p. 21) Choose the description of Christ in 1:1-4 that is most surprising or impactful to you. How should the statement you chose impact your perspective on how to live "in these last days" as one of Christ's followers?

**2. OBSERVE:** (question 11, p. 22) The author used seven different Old Testament passages to illustrate Christ's superiority to the angels. Based on what you know about his audience, why would this have been an effective strategy? What does his effective use of these passages tell you about the author?

**APPLY:** (question 13, p. 23) How can modern believers be guilty of giving misplaced attention—even worship—to the spiritual realm instead of to Christ? Why is it tempting to do so? Why is it dangerous?

**3. OBSERVE:** (question 17, p. 25) What three reasons are given in 2:3-4 to establish the credibility of our salvation? Note what New Testament event or occurrence they likely describe.

**APPLY:** (question 18, p. 25) In what ways are modern believers prone to drift away or neglect the truth we know? What regular practices might help us "pay much closer attention to what we have heard" (2:1a)?

**4. OBSERVE:** (question 21, p. 26) Why is it important for us to understand our salvation in family terms?

**APPLY:** (question 26, p. 27–28) Reread 2:8. How much does Jesus, who calls you part of His family, control? What area of your life feels most out of control? What news headline scares you the most? What sin feels unconquerable to you? How does the truth in 2:7-9 speak peace to your greatest fears?

5. **WRAP-UP:** (p. 28) What aspect of God's character has this week's passage of Hebrews shown you more clearly?

Fill in the following statement:

Knowing that God is _____ shows me that
I am _____.

What one step can you take this week to better live in light of this truth?

Teaching sessions available
for purchase or rent at
LifeWay.com/Better

WEEK TWO: BETTER THAN ANGELS     33

# Week Three:

## Better than Moses

Having established Jesus' superiority over angels in chapters 1–2, the author of Hebrews moved forward with his message of how the Old Testament finds its fulfillment in Christ. For the original Jewish Christian audience, no Old Testament prophet would have been more revered than Moses, a man entrusted by God with the responsibility to lead Israel out of bondage in Egypt, not to mention the responsibility of writing the Torah (the first five books of the Bible). Though just a man, Moses spoke face-to-face with God, receiving and administering the Law given at Mount Sinai. Because of Moses' enormous influence and lasting legacy, the author of Hebrews asked his hearers to "consider Jesus" in relation to Moses, pointing them to a better Deliverer (3:1b).

**READ THIS WEEK'S PASSAGE: HEBREWS 3:1–4:13**

1.  In 2–3 sentences, summarize the main ideas of the passage.

2.  According to this week's passage, who or what is Jesus Christ better than?

3.  Mark every occurrence of the word *Moses* in this week's section of the text with a red M. (Note: Joshua is Moses' successor, so mark his name as well.) How many occurrences did you find?

4.  Mark every occurrence of the word *therefore* and any synonyms for it, as you have previously, with a purple capital T and underline.

5.  How does this week's section of the text follow logically from the previous one? What previous idea is the *therefore* in 3:1 building on? Summarize it below.

## DAY TWO
### NOW LOOK MORE CLOSELY AT HEBREWS 3:1-6.

6. Look at 3:2. Specifically, what aspect of Moses' character is highlighted for comparison to Christ?

   "... just as Moses also was _____ in all God's house."

   Mark every occurrence of this word in 3:1-6 with **a wiggly green underline.**

7. What contrast are we given in 3:5-6 between Moses and Jesus?

   "_____ Moses was faithful _____ all God's house as a _____ ... "

   " ... _____ Christ is faithful _____ God's house as a _____."

   What distinction do you think the author wanted us to understand?

8. The author expanded on the idea of family we saw introduced last week in 2:10-18. He added the term *house* to his list of familial terms. As you did last week, mark every occurrence of *brothers* or *house* in this week's portion of the text with a blue underline.

9. What do you think is meant by the *if* statement in 3:6? Look up 2 Corinthians 13:5 to help with your answer.

10. Why might a contrast between Christ and Moses have been necessary and helpful for the original hearers of Hebrews?

11. **APPLY:** What great man or woman of faith have you placed on a pedestal? What are the dangers of believing or expecting that our leaders can "do no wrong"?

**NOW LOOK AT HEBREWS 3:7-19.**

12. What previous idea is the *therefore* in 3:7 building on? Summarize it below.

13. How many times is the word *today* repeated in this section of the text? What do you think the author wanted to emphasize?

14. The author of Hebrews quoted Psalm 95:7-11, referring to the forty years Israel wandered in the wilderness because of her disobedience. Look up Numbers 14:21-30 and answer the questions below.

    Who died in the wilderness without entering the promised land?

    What two men did enter the promised land (14:30)?

15. Note: Moses is not one of the names you wrote above, those who would enter the promised land. Look up Numbers 20:2-13 and record what you learn about him there.

    How does your answer reinforce the author's assertion that Jesus is greater than Moses?

16.  Compare Hebrews 3:6 with Hebrews 3:14. What repeated idea do you find?

17.  Note the continued repetition in 3:15. The Israelites who perished in the wilderness misplaced their confidence because of what heart condition?

18.  What reason does 3:18 give for Israel's inability to enter God's rest in the promised land?

     What reason does 3:19 give for Israel's inability to enter God's rest in the promised land?

19.  APPLY: In what current circumstance are you tempted to place your confidence in something or someone other than God? What area of hardness of heart might this be revealing in you?

**NOW LOOK AT HEBREWS 4:1-10.**

20. What previous idea is the *therefore* in 4:1 building on? Summarize it below.

21. What kind of fear do you think 4:1 is exhorting us to feel? Compare the NIV translation to help with your answer.

22. What good news do you think the Israelites heard that the New Testament Hebrews also heard (4:2)?

23. Old Testament Israel had the opportunity to enter into the physical rest of the promised land—a rest from their wandering and their enemies. We have the opportunity to enter into rest of a different nature. Look up Matthew 11:28-29 and note what Jesus has to say about our rest in the space below.

Based on what you wrote above, what work(s) do we rest from when we rest in Christ?

24. Having heard the good news, Israel did not enter God's rest because of disobedience. What did her disobedience reveal about her belief in the good news she had heard? Look up Matthew 13:18-23 to help with your answer.


25. **APPLY:** Our unbelief often manifests as some form of self-reliance. Think about your own life. What area of self-reliant unbelief keeps you from fully enjoying the rest granted to you in Christ?

**NOW LOOK AT HEBREWS 4:11-13.**

26. What previous idea is the *therefore* in 4:11 building on? Summarize it below.

27. Compare 4:11 in the ESV and the NIV. How does the NIV translate the word *strive*?

    What do you think this verse is exhorting us to do?

28. How do you think the summary statement in 4:11 connects to the next thoughts in 4:12-13?

29. What five descriptions are given for the Word of God in 4:12?

30. Hebrews 4:12 is probably familiar to you. It is often quoted to illustrate the power of God's Word to change us. How does reading this verse in context (particularly with its completing thought in v. 13) change or expand the way you understand its message?

31. **APPLY:** How have you known 4:12-13 to be true in your own experience? Describe a time when the Word of God divided you. What was the result?

## WRAP-UP

What aspect of God's character has this week's passage of Hebrews shown you more clearly?

Fill in the following statement:

Knowing that God is _____ shows me that I am _____.

What one step can you take this week to better live in light of this truth?

**INTRODUCTORY QUESTION:** Who do you look up to the most? Why?

1. **OBSERVE:** (question 10, p. 38) Why might a contrast between Christ and Moses have been necessary and helpful for the original hearers of Hebrews?

   **APPLY:** (question 11, p. 38) What great man or woman of faith have you placed on a pedestal? What are the dangers of believing or expecting that our leaders can "do no wrong"?

2. **OBSERVE:** (question 15, p. 39) How does Numbers 20:2-13 reinforce the author's assertion that Jesus is greater than Moses?

   **APPLY:** (question 19, p. 40) In what current circumstance are you tempted to place your confidence in something or someone other than God? What area of hardness of heart might this be revealing in you?

3. **OBSERVE:** (question 23, p. 41) Old Testament Israel had the opportunity to enter into the physical rest of the promised land—a rest from their wandering and their enemies. We have the opportunity to enter into rest of a different nature. Based on Matthew 11:28-29, what work(s) do we rest from when we rest in Christ?

   **APPLY:** (question 25, p. 42) Our unbelief often manifests as some form of self-reliance. Think about your own life. What area of self-reliant unbelief keeps you from fully enjoying the rest granted to you in Christ?

4. **OBSERVE:** (question 30, p. 43) Hebrews 4:12 is probably familiar to you. It is often quoted to illustrate the power of God's Word to change us. How does reading this verse in context (particularly with its completing thought in v. 13) change or expand the way you understand its message?

**APPLY:** (question 31, p. 44) How have you known 4:12-13 to be true in your own experience? Describe a time when the Word of God divided you. What was the result?

5. **WRAP-UP:** (p. 44) What aspect of God's character has this week's passage of Hebrews shown you more clearly?

Fill in the following statement:

Knowing that God is _____ shows me that
I am _____.

What one step can you take this week to better live in light of this truth?

## WEEK THREE | VIEWER GUIDE NOTES

# Week Four:

## Better High Priest

Last week we saw Jesus as better than Moses, leading us into a better rest. We were soberly warned to seek to enter that rest as obedient children.

This week we'll see the author of Hebrews develop the idea of Jesus as our Great High Priest, full of sympathy and mercy, in whom we can place our full confidence.

## DAY ONE

**READ THIS WEEK'S PASSAGE: HEBREWS 4:14–5:14.**

1. In 2–3 sentences, summarize the main ideas of the passage.

2. According to this week's passage, who or what is Jesus Christ better than?

3. Mark every occurrence of the words *high priest* in this week's section of the text with a red H. How many occurrences did you find?

4. Mark every occurrence of the word *therefore* and any synonyms for it, as you have previously, with a purple capital T and underline.

5. How does this week's section of the text follow logically from the previous one?

## NOW LOOK MORE CLOSELY AT HEBREWS 4:14-16.

6. Compare 4:14 in the NIV. What word does the verse begin with?


    If you have not done so already, mark it as you have elsewhere.


7. In 4:14 the idea of holding fast occurs as it has in two earlier verses. It will occur two more times in the Book of Hebrews as well. Fill in the blanks for what we are to hold fast to.

    3:6—" ... hold fast our _____ and

        our _____."

    3:14—" ... hold our original _____ firm to the end."

    4:14—" ... let us hold fast our _____."
        (See also 1 John 4:15.)

    6:18—" ... hold fast to the _____."

    10:23—" ... hold fast the _____
        without wavering ... "

Based on this comparison, to what should we hold fast? Be as specific as you can.


8. Look up the word *sympathize* in a dictionary or thesaurus, and write a definition for it below that best fits with the context of 4:15.
SYMPATHIZE:

9.   Christians affirm that Jesus was both fully God and fully man. How is the full humanity of Jesus emphasized in 4:15?

10.  Compare 4:15 in the NIV. In how many ways does it say Jesus was tempted as we are?

     How easy is it for you to believe this is true? Explain your answer.

     How important is it for you to believe this is true? Explain your answer.

11.  Why do you think the word *then* is included in 4:16? How might you mark it with your colored pencils, if you have not done so already?

12.  What attitude results in us when we recognize that Jesus can sympathize with us when we are tempted (4:16)?

13.  APPLY: What temptation are you currently battling that you want to believe is unique to you and impossible to resist? How should you pray with confidence about that temptation?

## NOW LOOK AT HEBREWS 5:1-6.

14. What two duties is every high priest expected to perform (5:1)?

15. What comparisons did the author make in this section between the Old Testament priesthood and the priesthood of Jesus?

| | OLD TESTAMENT HIGH PRIEST | CHRIST, OUR GREAT HIGH PRIEST |
|---|---|---|
| Receives calling from whom | (5:4) | |
| Is beset by weakness? (Yes/No) | | |
| Offers sacrifices for whom | | |
| Holds office for how long | | |

16. Why is it important that a high priest is called by God versus achieving or being elected to the role (5:4)?

17. In 5:5-6, the author quoted Psalm 2:7 and Psalm 110:4. Look up Psalm 2:6-7 and note what title verse 6 gives for Jesus, before describing Him as a Son in verse 7.

We will save a full discussion of Melchizedek until Week Six of our study. For now, look up Genesis 14:18 and note what two titles are given there for him. How do his two titles prefigure (shadow or point to) Christ?

18. Why might a contrast between Christ and the high priest of the temple have been necessary and helpful for the original hearers of Hebrews?

19. APPLY: With Christ as our Great High Priest, all believers are called to serve as a royal priesthood (1 Pet. 2:9). How good are you at dealing "gently with the ignorant and wayward" God places in your sphere of influence? How might you grow in that regard (5:2a)?

**NOW LOOK AT HEBREWS 5:7-10.**

20. Look up Matthew 26:36-39, Jesus' tearful prayer to the Father in Gethsemane. How did the Father answer Jesus' request in verse 39?

21. The author said Jesus "was heard because of his reverence" (Heb. 5:7). What does it mean that God hears our prayers? What does it not mean?

22. In the Week Two teaching we discussed that Jesus was made perfect through suffering (2:10 and also 5:9) in the sense that He completed the perfect work God had ordained for Him. What do you think it means that Jesus "learned obedience through what he suffered" (5:8)? What can it not mean?

23. Why do you think 5:9 says Christ "became the source of eternal salvation to all who obey him"? What relationship does our obedience have to our salvation? Look up 1 John 2:3-6 to help with your answer.

24. **APPLY:** How has God allowed you to learn obedience through suffering? What wrong attitudes or behaviors has He allowed suffering to teach you to cease? What right attitudes or behaviors did you learn to practice in their place?

## NOW LOOK AT HEBREWS 5:11-14.

25. How would you characterize the author's tone in this section? Why do you think he took this tone?

26. What practice does 5:12 indicate is a mark of spiritual maturity?

27. What kind of teaching do you think the author had in view in 5:12? Check the best answer.

_____ Exercising a teaching gift in front of a room full of people
_____ Passing on the basics of our faith to another person

28. In the chart below, note every contrasting description you can find in 5:11-14.

| THE IMMATURE BELIEVER | THE MATURE BELIEVER |
| --- | --- |
| Dull of hearing (v. 11) | |

29. What two examples of "milk" (basic principles) should all believers understand as soon as possible in the maturation process?

30. What two examples of "solid food" should mature (or maturing) believers strive to understand?

31. What powers are we to train by constant practice (5:14)?

32. Look up the word *discern* in a dictionary or thesaurus, and write a definition for *discernment* below that best fits with the context of 5:14.
DISCERNMENT:

33. What tool is essential for training in discernment? Look back at Hebrews 4:12 to help with your answer.

34. APPLY: In what one area of your life has your discernment grown? How have you learned to be better at discerning good from evil?

In what one area of your life do you need more discernment? What steps can you take to grow in this area?

WRAP-UP

What aspect of God's character has this week's passage of Hebrews shown you more clearly?

Fill in the following statement:

Knowing that God is _____ shows me that I am _____.

What one step can you take this week to better live in light of this truth?

**INTRODUCTORY QUESTION:** What food item are you unable to resist, no matter how hard you try?

1. **OBSERVE:** (question 10, p. 54) Compare 4:15 in the NIV. In how many ways does it say Jesus was tempted as we are? How easy is it for you to believe this is true? How important is it for you to believe this is true? Explain your answers.

   **APPLY:** (question 13, p. 54) What temptation are you currently battling that you want to believe is unique to you and impossible to resist? How should you pray with confidence about that temptation?

2. **OBSERVE:** (question 18, p. 56) Why might a contrast between Christ and the high priest of the temple have been necessary and helpful for the original hearers of Hebrews?

   **APPLY:** (question 19, p. 56) With Christ as our Great High Priest, all believers are called to serve as a royal priesthood (1 Pet. 2:9). How good are you at dealing "gently with the ignorant and wayward" God places in your sphere of influence? How might you grow in that regard (5:2a)?

3. **OBSERVE:** (question 22, p. 57) What do you think it means that Jesus "learned obedience through what he suffered" (5:8)? What can it not mean?

   **APPLY:** (question 24, p. 58) How has God allowed you to learn obedience through suffering? What wrong attitudes or behaviors has He allowed suffering to teach you to cease? What right attitudes or behaviors did you learn to practice in their place?

4. **OBSERVE:** (question 33, p. 60) What tool is essential for training in discernment? Look back at Hebrews 4:12 to help with your answer.

APPLY: (question 34, pp. 60-61) In what one area of your life has your discernment grown? How have you learned to be better at discerning good from evil? In what one area of your life do you need more discernment? What steps can you take to grow in this area?

5. WRAP-UP: (p. 61) What aspect of God's character has this week's passage of Hebrews shown you more clearly?

Fill in the following statement:

Knowing that God is _____ shows me that
I am _____.

What one step can you take this week to better live in light of this truth?

## WEEK FOUR | VIEWER GUIDE NOTES

Teaching sessions available
for purchase or rent at
LifeWay.com/Better

WEEK FOUR: BETTER HIGH PRIEST        65

# Week Five:

## Better Promise

Remember to take time some time this week for your repetitive reading through the Book of Hebrews. Choose a short passage that stands out to you. Copy it into the front of your Bible study book and begin committing it to memory.

Last week we explored the significance of Jesus as our better High Priest, a theme the author will revisit and expand upon as we move through the next five chapters.

This week we receive assurance that we have been given a better promise than even Abraham himself received. Ours is a promise of salvation, guaranteed by the oath of the Most High God, a hope that is anchored by the finished work of Christ on our behalf.

**READ THIS WEEK'S PASSAGE: HEBREWS 6:1-20.**

1.  In 2–3 sentences, summarize the main ideas of the passage.

2.  Each week we have reflected on Jesus as better than someone or something else that preceded Him. What "better than" comparisons are made in this week's passage? See 6:9 and 6:16 to help with your answer.

3.  Continue your annotating as in previous weeks:
    - Mark every occurrence of the word *therefore* and any synonyms for it, as you have previously, with **a purple capital T and <u>underline</u>**.
    - Mark the occurrence of the words *high priest* in this week's section of the text with **<u>a red H</u>**.

4.  How does this week's section of the text follow logically from the previous one? What previous idea is the *therefore* in 6:1 building on? Summarize it below.

## NOW LOOK MORE CLOSELY AT HEBREWS 6:1-3.

5.  What seems to be the problem in 6:1-3? What action do you think the author wanted his hearers to take?

6.  The author drew his readers' attention to six "foundational" teachings. Write each below as it is worded in the text, and then explain what you think it refers to.

    1.

    2.

    3.

    4.

    5.

    6.

7. Compare the phrase, "Therefore let us leave the elementary doctrine of Christ" (6:1a) to the language in the NIV. Do you think the author wanted us to completely set aside these six teachings?

8. Knowing that the letter's primary original audience was the Hebrews (Jewish converts to Christianity), where would they have first learned an "elementary doctrine of Christ" that had not led them to maturity? Look up John 5:39-40,46 to help with your answer.

9. **APPLY:** What fears or misconceptions keep believers from moving beyond foundational truths to maturity? How susceptible are you to getting stuck in the ditch of spiritual immaturity?

## DAY THREE
### NOW LOOK AT HEBREWS 6:4-8.

10. These five verses have been the source of much controversy. We will discuss them during the teaching time. For now, give them a close read and consider their context. Then check the interpretation you think fits best.

_____ The passage teaches it is possible to lose your salvation.

_____ The passage gives a hypothetical situation to illustrate the folly of turning from the gospel.

_____ The passage describes those who come in contact with the gospel, hear its call to repentance, but ultimately turn from it unrepentant.

**List any cross-references you know of to support the answer you chose above.**

11. How are true believers who grow to maturity like the land described in 6:7?

12. How are those who give only an outward appearance of belief like the land described in 6:8?

13. Look up Isaiah 55:10-13 and note how it amplifies your understanding of Hebrews 6:7-8.

14. Summarize the main point of 6:4-8 into one sentence.

15. **APPLY:** How should the warning of 6:4-8 shape the way the believer regards sin, particularly habitual sin? What should be the believer's response to this passage?

## DAY FOUR
### NOW LOOK AT HEBREWS 6:9-12.

16. What was the author's attitude toward his hearers in 6:9? Mark the word *better* with a yellow highlighter. It will start to appear with some regularity for the rest of the letter.


What are some examples of "things that belong to salvation" (6:9b)?


17. What attribute of God did the author note in 6:10 to encourage his hearers?


What visible evidences of his hearers' salvation did he cite?


18. Compare 6:11-12 in the ESV and the NIV. What word does the NIV use for *sluggish*?


What does this imply is necessary if we are to imitate "those who ... inherit the promises" (6:12b)?

19. What do you think the author wanted his hearers to do? Rewrite 6:11-12 in your own words using as few words as possible to capture his meaning.

20. What two practices enable us to inherit what has been promised to us (6:12)? Write them below and describe why each is necessary in the life of the believer.

    1.


    2.


21. Based on what the letter has covered thus far and what it will cover in the remainder of chapter 6, what people would its Hebrew listeners have thought of as worthy of imitation?


22. **APPLY:** Think of someone God has placed in your life whose example is worth imitating. How has that person been an example of faith and patience to you? How has that person modeled the hard work of pursuing maturity?

## DAY FIVE

**NOW LOOK AT HEBREWS 6:13-20.**

23. What imitation-worthy example of faith and patience is given in this passage?

24. Look up Genesis 22:17 and read its context to find out at what point in Abraham's story God spoke the promise quoted in 6:14. Note what you find below.

25. According to 6:16, why do people swear oaths to seal a promise? Restate the central thought in your own words.

    **Describe a time you have done this. Did the oath help you keep your word?**

26. According to 6:17-18, why did God swear an oath to seal His promise?

27. What are the "two unchangeable things" referred to in 6:18? (Hint: they are discussed in 6:13-17.)

28. "The inner place behind the curtain" refers to the holy of holies in the temple, entered only once a year by the high priest to make atonement for the sins of the people (6:19b). Why do you think the author said our hope is anchored there specifically?

29. In the space below, sketch a picture of a boat on an ocean that has dropped anchor into solid rock. Label each part of your picture to help you fully grasp the metaphor.

30. **APPLY:** How is an anchor an apt metaphor for the hope we have
    in the God of our salvation? How has your faith been an anchor
    for you personally?

## WRAP-UP

What aspect of God's character has this week's passage of Hebrews shown
you more clearly?

Fill in the following statement:

Knowing that God is _____ shows me that
I am _____.

What one step can you take this week to better live in light of this
truth?

## WEEK FIVE | GROUP DISCUSSION

**INTRODUCTORY QUESTION:** What is the best common sense advice you've ever received?

**1. OBSERVE:** (question 6, p. 69) The author drew his readers' attention to six "foundational" teachings in 6:1-3. Look at each as it is worded in the text, and then explain what you think it refers to.

**APPLY:** (question 9, p. 70) What fears or misconceptions keep believers from moving beyond foundational truths to maturity? How susceptible are you to getting stuck in the ditch of spiritual immaturity?

**2. OBSERVE:** (question 14, p. 72) Summarize the main point of 6:4-8 into one sentence.

**APPLY:** (question 15, p. 72) How should the warning of 6:4-8 shape the way the believer regards sin, particularly habitual sin? What should be the believer's response to this passage?

**3. OBSERVE:** (question 19, p. 74) What do you think the author wanted his hearers to do? Rewrite 6:11-12 in your own words using as few words as possible to capture his meaning.

**APPLY:** (question 22, p. 74) Think of someone God has placed in your life whose example is worth imitating. How has that person been an example of faith and patience to you? How has that person modeled the hard work of pursuing maturity?

**4. OBSERVE:** (question 29, p. 76) Discuss your picture of a boat on an ocean that has dropped anchor into solid rock. How did you label each part of your picture to help you fully grasp the metaphor?

**APPLY:** (question 30, p. 76) How is an anchor an apt metaphor for the hope we have in the God our salvation? How has your faith been an anchor for you personally?

5. **WRAP-UP:** (p. 77) What aspect of God's character has this week's passage of Hebrews shown you more clearly?

Fill in the following statement:

Knowing that God is _____ shows me that I am _____.

What one step can you take this week to better live in light of this truth?

# Week Six:

## Better Hope and Covenant

Last week we savored the certainty of our right standing with God, secured by Jesus. This week it's finally time to nail down the connection between Jesus and the shadowy figure of Melchizedek, whom we first met in Hebrews 5, whose story is found in Genesis 14:17-18 and Psalm 110:4. Thus far we've seen Melchizedek's name mentioned three times in the Book of Hebrews. We'll see six more references to him in this week's passage. It seems the author of Hebrews wanted to draw our attention to a specific connection with this ancient priest-king of Genesis.

**READ THIS WEEK'S PASSAGE: HEBREWS 7:1–8:13.**

1.  In 2–3 sentences, summarize the main ideas of the passage.

2.  What "better than" comparisons are made in this week's passage? List as many as you can find.

3.  Continue your annotating as in previous weeks:
    ☐ Mark every occurrence of the words *high priest* in this week's section of the text with **a red H**.
    ☐ Mark every occurrence of the word *covenant* in this week's section of the text with **a red C**.
    ☐ Mark every occurrence of the word *better* in this week's section of the text with **a yellow highlighter**.

4.  How does this week's section of the text follow logically from the previous one?

**NOW LOOK MORE CLOSELY AT HEBREWS 7:1-10.**

The author's logic can be difficult to trace in this section of the text. Do your best to answer the questions below. We will spend time clarifying our thinking during the teaching.

5. Look up the following prophecies about Christ and compare the titles you find there to those given to Melchizedek in 7:1-2.

   **Isaiah 9:6-7**


   **Jeremiah 23:5-6**


6. Scan Genesis 14:17-18 and note any additional possible parallels between Christ and Melchizedek.



7. In 7:3 do you think the author was speaking literally or figuratively? Explain your answer.



8. Abraham is the "original Hebrew," the founding father of the nation of Israel. What do you think the author wanted us to recognize in 7:4?


   **How did he go on to make this point in 7:5-10? List every evidence he gave to support his claim.**

9.  What contrast did the author make between the levitical priesthood and Melchizedek's priesthood in 7:4-10? How is Melchizedek's better?

10. In 7:8 who do you think is meant by "one of whom it is testified that he lives"? Look up John 11:25 to help with your answer.

11. What point do you think the author wanted us to understand in 7:9-10? Rewrite these two verses in your own words.

12. **APPLY:** The Bible highlights the practice of tithing because the way we give and spend our money often reveals the state of our hearts. If your bank statement were made public, what (or who) would it reveal you show honor to? What would it reveal you believe to be a source of blessing?

## DAY THREE
### NOW LOOK AT HEBREWS 7:11-19.

13. The author returned to the idea of perfection that he introduced earlier in his letter. In your copy of the text, mark every occurrence of the word *perfect* or *perfection* in chapter 7 with an orange P and underline. Mark also its previous occurrences in 2:10 and 5:9.

14. What do you think the author wanted us to understand was imperfect (7:11)?

    What do you think he wanted us to understand is perfect (7:15-17)?

15. Having compared the levitical priesthood with that of Melchizedek, the author then addressed a silent objection his hearers would have raised regarding Jesus' line of descent. What is it?

    By law, priests had to be descended from the tribe of
    _____ (7:11).

    Jesus, however, was descended from the tribe of
    _____ (7:14).

16. How did the author characterize this change to the priesthood (7:18-19)? Explain the contrast between good and better that he set up in these verses.

17. Specifically, in what way does the priesthood of Christ introduce a better hope to the believer (7:19b)? (See also 7:24.)

18. **APPLY:** Prior to the perfect high priesthood of Christ, only the levitical priests could draw near to God—and then only once a year with trembling. How should the reality of our blood-bought nearness to God impact the way we think about our sin? About our suffering?

**NOW LOOK AT HEBREWS 7:20-28.**

19. What contrasts between the priesthoods of Christ and of Levi do you find in 7:20-28? In the chart below, note everything you can find and infer.

| CHRIST | LEVI |
| --- | --- |
|  |  |

20. The author returned to the significance of the oath mentioned in Hebrews 6:17 and Psalm 110:4. What kind of covenant does the oath ensure (7:22)?

21. What is Jesus' role with regard to that covenant (7:22)?

Look up the word *guarantor* in a dictionary or thesaurus, and write a definition for it below that fits with the context.

GUARANTOR:

22. In 7:23-25 what "therefore" idea is communicated?

What do you think it means that Christ is "able to save to the uttermost" (7:25a)? Compare it in the NIV to help with your answer.

23. What does the eternal Christ live to do for us (7:25)?

Look up the simple verb form of the word *intercession* in a dictionary or thesaurus, and write a definition for it below that fits with the context.

INTERCEDE:

24. Prior to the new covenant under Christ, what had to be done by law to address the sins of "men in their weakness" (7:28a)? Read the passages below and note the situations requiring each of the two sacrifices described.

Leviticus 4:3-12

Leviticus 4:13-21

25. In Hebrews 7:18 the author referred to the weakness and uselessness of the Old Testament law. How does your answer to the previous question support his description?

26. **APPLY**: How would the message of the superior high priesthood of Christ encourage the original hearers of Hebrews from falling back into old patterns of worship? How should it encourage us?

## NOW LOOK AT HEBREWS 8:1-13.

27. How is Jesus' current location "better" than that of any earthly priest (8:1)?

28. The Jews regarded the tabernacle (and later the temple) as the place where heaven touched earth, where God met with man. What do you think the author wanted his hearers to understand about the tabernacle as it relates to heaven (8:2-6)?

29. How does the beautiful prophecy of Jeremiah 31:31-34 (as quoted in 8:8-12) reinforce the author's message of that which was incomplete or imperfect and that which is better?

30. Specifically, how does Jeremiah say the new covenant will be better than the old one? In the chart below, paraphrase each way the new covenant is better in the right-hand column next to the verse noted. Then write a contrasting statement that describes how the old covenant was incomplete or imperfect.

| OLD COVENANT (INCOMPLETE/IMPERFECT) | NEW COVENANT (BETTER) |
| --- | --- |
| | Hebrews 8:10a |
| | Hebrews 8:10b |
| | Hebrews 8:11 |
| | Hebrews 8:12 |

31. Look up the word *obsolete* in a dictionary or thesaurus and write a definition for it below that best fits the context of 8:13.
OBSOLETE:

Now write 8:13 in your own words.

32. APPLY: Copy the words of 8:12 in the space below.

What sin in your past is difficult to forget? What response toward God should the truth of this verse cause in us? What response toward those who sin against us should it cause?

## WRAP-UP

What aspect of God's character has this week's passage of Hebrews shown you more clearly?

Fill in the following statement:

Knowing that God is _____ shows me that I am _____.

What one step can you take this week to better live in light of this truth?

**INTRODUCTORY QUESTION:** What is your favorite place on the planet?

1. **OBSERVE:** (question 9, p. 86) What contrast did the author make between the levitical priesthood and Melchizedek's priesthood in 7:4-10? How is Melchizedek's better?

   **APPLY:** (question 12, p. 86) The Bible highlights the practice of tithing because the way we give and spend our money often reveals the state of our hearts. If your bank statement were made public, what (or who) would it reveal you show honor to? What would it reveal you believe to be a source of blessing?

2. **OBSERVE:** (question 17, p. 88) Specifically, in what way does the priesthood of Christ introduce a better hope to the believer (7:19b)? (See also 7:24.)

   **APPLY:** (question 18, p. 88) Prior to the perfect high priesthood of Christ, only the levitical priests could draw near to God—and then only once a year with trembling. How should the reality of our blood-bought nearness to God impact the way we think about our sin? About our suffering?

3. **OBSERVE:** (question 22, p. 90) In 7:23-25 what "therefore" idea is communicated? What do you think it means that Christ is "able to save to the uttermost" (7:25a)? Compare it in the NIV to help with your answer.

   **APPLY:** (question 26, p. 91) How would the message of the superior high priesthood of Christ encourage the original hearers of Hebrews from falling back into old patterns of worship? How should it encourage us?

4. **OBSERVE:** (question 27, p. 92) How is Jesus' current location "better" than that of any earthly priest (8:1)?

**APPLY:** (question 32, p. 94) Reflecting on 8:12, what sin in your past is difficult to forget? What response toward God should the truth of this verse cause in us? What response toward those who sin against us should it cause?

5. **WRAP-UP:** (p. 94) What aspect of God's character has this week's passage of Hebrews shown you more clearly?

Fill in the following statement:
Knowing that God is _____ shows me that
I am _____.

What one step can you take this week to better live in light of this truth?

# WEEK SIX | VIEWER GUIDE NOTES

Teaching sessions available
for purchase or rent at
LifeWay.com/Better

WEEK SIX: BETTER HOPE AND COVENANT    99

# Week Seven:

## Better Tabernacle

Remember to take time this week to read repetitively and to work on memorizing the passage you copied into the front of your Bible study book.

Last week we were shown Jesus Christ as the Mediator of a new and better covenant, serving as our Great High Priest. This week we see shadows turned to realities. Our Great High Priest has done what no other priest could by offering Himself as a better sacrifice, thereby granting us access to the true and better tabernacle.

**READ THIS WEEK'S PASSAGE: HEBREWS 9:1-28.**

1.  In 2–3 sentences, summarize the main ideas of the passage.

2.  What "better than" comparisons are made in this week's passage?

3.  Continue your annotating as in previous weeks:

    ☐ Mark every occurrence of the words *high priest* in this week's section of the text with **a red H**.

    ☐ Mark every occurrence of the word *covenant* in this week's section of the text with **a red C**.

    ☐ Mark *therefore* and any synonyms for it in your copy of the text with **a purple capital T and underline**.

    ☐ Mark every occurrence of the word *better* in this week's section of the text with **a yellow highlighter**.

    ☐ Mark every occurrence of the word *blood* in chapter 9 with **a red B and underline**.

4.  How does this week's section of the text follow logically from the previous one?

**NOW LOOK MORE CLOSELY AT HEBREWS 9:1-10.**

5.  In 9:1 what word did the author use to describe the "place of holiness"?

    Look back at 8:5. What was God's intent for the earthly tabernacle and the old covenant?

6.  Below is a diagram of the tabernacle (or tent) described in 9:1-8. Mark the following things on the diagram:

    ☐  Find the first section of the tabernacle (9:2) and shade it **green**.

    ☐  Above the diagram, label the first section with its name.

    ☐  Find the second section of the tabernacle (9:3-5) and shade it **orange**.

    ☐  Above the diagram, label the second section with its name.

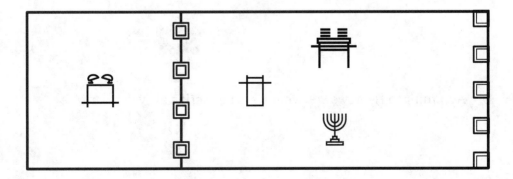

7.  Look at 9:7 and answer the following questions:

Who could go into the most holy place?

How often could he go into the most holy place?

What was required to access the most holy place?

8.  Look up Leviticus 16, a chapter describing the particular day the author of Hebrews referred to in 9:7. What "once a year" day was he referencing?

Read Leviticus 16:2. Why is the most holy place such a significant location?

9.  According to Hebrews 9:9, what was the sacrificial system unable to do?

Look up the word *conscience* in a dictionary or thesaurus and write a definition for it below that best fits the context of 9:9.
CONSCIENCE:

10. APPLY: How does a better understanding of the ritual system of the old covenant heighten our gratitude for the work of Christ in establishing the new covenant?

**NOW LOOK AT HEBREWS 9:11-14.**

11. What do you think the author meant by "good things that have come" (9:11)? Based on your study of Hebrews thus far, give three examples of good things that have come because of Christ.

    1.

    2.

    3.

12. Christ, the better Sacrifice, is given through a better tent. What is that better, or more perfect, tent the author of Hebrews was speaking of? Look ahead to 9:24 to help you with your answer.

13. The author gave us four proofs that Christ is a better sacrifice than the animals sacrificed under the old covenant system. Fill in the chart below contrasting the two sacrifices.

| ANIMAL SACRIFICES (INCOMPLETE/IMPERFECT) | JESUS (BETTER) |
| --- | --- |
| They were made every year. | 9:12a |
| Their blood gave partial redemption. | 9:12b |
| They were without external/ physical blemish. | 9:14b |
| They were unable to perfect the conscience. | 9:14b |

14. In 9:12 the author told us the blood of Christ secures for us an "eternal redemption." *Redeem* and *ransom* are also used throughout the Bible to convey the same idea. Look up the following verses and note what Christ has redeemed or ransomed us from.

    Titus 2:14

    1 Peter 1:18

15. Now look at 9:14. Considering what you noted above, what might the author of Hebrews have meant by saying the sacrifice of Christ would "purify our conscience from dead works to serve the living God" (9:14b)?

16. APPLY: Sometimes, even as believers whose sins have been forgiven, we can continue to live under the weight of a guilty conscience for our past or ongoing failures. What sin weighs heavy on your conscience even though you know it is forgiven? How is a guilty conscience keeping you from serving the living God?

**NOW LOOK AT HEBREWS 9:15-22.**

17. What previous idea is the *therefore* in 9:15 building on? Summarize it below.

18. What role does Christ play in the initiation of the new covenant (9:15)?

Look up the verb form of the word *mediator* in a dictionary or thesaurus, and write a definition for it below.
MEDIATE:

Now look up 1 Timothy 2:5. Between what two parties is Christ the mediator?
" ... between _____ and _____ ... "

19. What legal image did the author use in Hebrews 9:16-17?

How does this image help you understand the necessity of Christ's death in establishing the new covenant?

20. In 9:18-21 the author summarized the events of Exodus 24:3-8. He did so to help us understand Christ's covenantal role in relation to Moses'. Read the Exodus account. What role did Moses play between God and the Israelites by giving them the law?

What specific act (mentioned in both Hebrews and Exodus) demonstrated this role?

21. Which biblical principle regarding blood is stated in Hebrews 9:22?

Look up Leviticus 17:11. What reason is given for this principle?

22. APPLY: Through His shed blood, Christ has mediated peace between God and man. In fact, *peacemaker* is a synonym for *mediator*. Read Matthew 5:9. How should those sprinkled by the blood of the Great Mediator be imitators of Him?

Specifically, which of your primary relationships most needs you to be a peacemaker? In what way?

**NOW LOOK AT HEBREWS 9:23-28.**

23. According to 9:23-24, what level of access did Christ's better sacrifice secure for Him (and for us)?

24. Specifically, what work is Jesus doing now on our behalf as He abides in the presence of God? Look back at your homework for Week Six, question 23 on page 90 (Heb. 7:25).

25. Here again we see a contrast in the sacrifice of Jesus compared to the sacrifice of the old covenant high priest. In the chart below, mark a ✓ in the box indicating who accomplished each item, and mark an X in the box indicating who did not.

|  | OLD COVENANT HIGH PRIEST | JESUS CHRIST |
|---|---|---|
| Appeared face-to-face in the presence of the Lord (See Lev. 16:11-13 to help with your answer.) |  |  |
| Personally suffered to provide the required sacrifice |  |  |
| Entered heaven itself |  |  |

26. According to 9:26 when Jesus provided a much better sacrifice than the yearly animal sacrifice, what was the result?

27. How does 9:27-28 tell us Christ's work will be ultimately finished?

What word describes the way believers are to wait?

28. **APPLY:** Is eagerness for the return of Christ merely a state of mind? How should our eagerness for Christ's return translate into action?

What fears or sinful desires threaten to diminish your eagerness for His return? List two below and confess them in prayer.

## WRAP-UP

What aspect of God's character has this week's passage of Hebrews shown you more clearly?

Fill in the following statement:.

Knowing that God is _____ shows me that
I am _____.

What one step can you take this week to better live in light of this truth?

**INTRODUCTORY QUESTION:** What is the dumbest argument you have ever had?

**1. OBSERVE:** (question 8, p. 104) Look up Leviticus 16, a chapter describing the particular day the author of Hebrews referred to in 9:7. What "once a year" day was he referencing? Read Leviticus 16:2. Why is the most holy place such a significant location?

**APPLY:** (question 10, p. 105) How does a better understanding of the ritual system of the old covenant heighten our gratitude for the work of Christ in establishing the new covenant?

**2. OBSERVE:** (question 15, p. 107) What might the author of Hebrews have meant by saying the sacrifice of Christ would "purify our conscience from dead works to serve the living God" (9:14b)?

**APPLY:** (question 16, p. 107) Sometimes, even as believers whose sins have been forgiven, we can continue to live under the weight of a guilty conscience for our past or ongoing failures. What sin weighs heavy on your conscience even though you know it is forgiven? How is a guilty conscience keeping you from serving the living God?

**3. OBSERVE:** (question 18, p. 108) What role does Christ play in the initiation of the New Covenant (9:15)? Look up the verb form of that word in a dictionary or thesaurus, and write a definition for it. Now look up 1 Timothy 2:5. Between what two parties is Christ the mediator?

**APPLY:** (question 22, p. 109) Through His shed blood, Christ has mediated peace between God and man. In fact, *peacemaker* is a synonym for *mediator*. Read Matthew 5:9. How should those sprinkled by the blood of the Great Mediator be imitators of Him? Specifically, which of your primary relationships most needs you to be a peacemaker? In what way?

4. **OBSERVE:** (question 27, p. 111) How does 9:27-28 tell us Christ's work will be ultimately finished? What word describes the way believers are to wait?

**APPLY:** (question 28, p. 111) Is eagerness for the return of Christ merely a state of mind? How should our eagerness for Christ's return translate into action? What fears or sinful desires threaten to diminish your eagerness for His return?

5. **WRAP-UP:** (p. 112) What aspect of God's character has this week's passage of Hebrews shown you more clearly?

Fill in the following statement:

Knowing that God is _____ shows me that I am _____.

What one step can you take this week to better live in light of this truth?

Teaching sessions available
for purchase or rent at
LifeWay.com/Better

WEEK SEVEN: BETTER TABERNACLE     117

# Week Eight:

## Better Sacrifice

Abraham, Moses, Melchizedek, the tabernacle, the priesthood, the high priest, the animal sacrifices: all of these pointed toward a greater truth than themselves. If the Old Testament is a well-furnished room cloaked in shadows, the New Testament flips on the lights.[1] As the author drew his comparisons to a close, he emphasized the permanence of Christ's better sacrifice, exhorting his hearers to respond in faith, hope, love, and obedience.

1.  Benjamin Breckinridge Warfield, *The Works of Benjamin B. Warfield: Volume II, Biblical Doctrines* (Oxford, UK: Oxford University Press, 1932), 142. Retrieved from https://app.wordsearchbible.com, accessed on August 26, 2019.

**READ THIS WEEK'S PASSAGE: HEBREWS 10:1-39.**

1. In 2–3 sentences, summarize the main ideas of the passage.

2. What "better than" comparisons are made in this week's passage?

3. Continue your annotating as in previous weeks:
   - Mark every occurrence of the word *covenant* in this week's section of the text with **a red C**.
   - Mark *therefore* and any synonyms for it in your copy of the text with **a purple capital T and underline**.
   - Mark every occurrence of the word *better* in this week's section of the text with **a yellow highlighter**.
   - Mark every occurrence of the word *perfect* or *perfection* with **an orange P and underline**.
   - Mark every occurrence of *a familial term* (sons, brothers, children) with **a blue underline**.
   - Mark every occurrence of the word *faithful* with **a wiggly green underline**.

4. How does this week's section of the text follow logically from the previous one?

## NOW LOOK MORE CLOSELY AT HEBREWS 10:1-10.

5.  What did the author say the law (old covenant) was unable to do?

    10:1

    10:4

6.  What purpose did the author say the law served?

    10:1

    10:3

7.  In 10:5-10 the author referenced Psalm 40. Describe the distinction he made between the temple sacrifices and the sacrifice of Christ.

8.  If God took no pleasure in sacrifices and offerings, why do you think He would command that they be made? Give your best answer.

9.  APPLY: The original hearers of Hebrews were tempted to return to empty practices as a means of pleasing God. What "sacrifices and offerings" do you think modern believers are most tempted to believe God takes pleasure in (v. 5b)?

**NOW LOOK AT HEBREWS 10:11-18.**

10. What contrast is made in 10:11-14?

11. In 10:12 we read the third of four times the Book of Hebrews speaks of Christ sitting down. (See also Hebrews 1:3; 8:1; 12:2.) What do you think is the significance of these repeated mentions?

12. In 10:13 we are told what Christ is doing as He sits. What is it?

    **When do you think "that time until his enemies should be made a footstool for his feet" refers to?**

13. In 10:16 the author again quoted Jeremiah 31:33. What significant difference between the old and new covenants does this prophecy indicate? Compare Exodus 34:1 to help with your answer.

14. How is having a covenant written on hearts and minds better than having a covenant written on stone?

15. Paraphrasing Jeremiah 31:34, the author pointed out another way the new covenant is better than the old. What is it (10:17)?

What becomes unnecessary as a result (10:18)?

16. **APPLY:** Describe a time when the Holy Spirit brought to mind words of truth in the midst of temptation or sin. How is having an internal, Spirit-given sense of right and wrong better than having an external one?

**NOW LOOK AT HEBREWS 10:19-31.**

17. What previous idea is the *therefore* in 10:19 building on? Summarize it below.

18. What confidence does the new covenant give us that the old covenant could not (10:19)?

19. Paraphrase the main points of 10:19-25 by completing the following statements in your own words:

10:19—Since ...

10:21—And since ...

10:22—Let us ...

10:23—Let us ...

10:24—Let us ...

10:25—Let us ...

10:25—Let us ...

20. Compare 6:1-5 to 10:26-31. What similar argument is being presented?

21. In a letter that seeks to establish how much better Christ is than the Old Testament shadows that pointed to Him, what kind of contrast is made in 10:28-29?

22. Note each description given in 10:29 for the person who "[goes] on sinning deliberately" (v. 26a).

    He has _____.

    He has _____.

    He has _____.

23. What kind of sin do you think fits the descriptions you noted above?

24. What attribute of God will be experienced by those who reject the truth (10:30-31)?

25. **APPLY:** Which of the "let us" statements of 10:22-25 is easiest for you to obey? Which one is the hardest for you? Why?

**NOW LOOK AT HEBREWS 10:32-39.**

26. What do the details mentioned in 10:32-34 reveal about the past experiences of the original audience? Note what you learn about:

Their past circumstances:

Their past attitudes:

Their past faith:

27. What have these past experiences granted that must not be thrown away (10:35)?

How will this serve them as they look toward the future (10:36)?

28. How did the prophecy from Habakkuk 2:3-4 (quoted in 10:37-38) reinforce the author's message?

29. Based on the context of the chapter, what does it mean to "[shrink] back" (v. 38a)?

30. **APPLY:** How has a past difficult circumstance taught you joy and strengthened your faith?

31. How does "[recalling] the former days" help you to face a current situation or quell fears about the future (10:32)?

## WRAP-UP

What aspect of God's character has this week's passage of Hebrews shown you more clearly?

Fill in the following statement:

Knowing that God is _____ shows me that I am _____.

What one step can you take this week to better live in light of this truth?

## WEEK EIGHT | GROUP DISCUSSION

**INTRODUCTORY QUESTION:** What is the most valuable possession you have ever broken or lost?

1. **OBSERVE:** (question 8, p. 121) If God took no pleasure in sacrifices and offerings, why do you think He would command that they be made? Give your best answer.

   **APPLY:** (question 9, p. 121) The original hearers of Hebrews were tempted to return to empty practices as a means of pleasing God. What "sacrifices and offerings" do you think modern believers are most tempted to believe God takes pleasure in (v. 5b)?

2. **OBSERVE:** (question 14, p. 122) How is having a covenant written on hearts and minds better than having a covenant written on stone?

   **APPLY:** (question 16, p. 123) Describe a time when the Holy Spirit brought to mind words of truth in the midst of temptation or sin. How is having an internal, Spirit-given sense of right and wrong better than having an external one?

3. **OBSERVE:** (question 19, p. 124) Paraphrase the main points of 10:19-25 in your own words.

   **APPLY:** (question 25, p. 125) Which of the "let us" statements of 10:22-25 is easiest for you to obey? Which one is the hardest for you? Why?

4. **OBSERVE:** (question 29, p. 126) Based on the context of the chapter, what does it mean to "[shrink] back" (v. 38a)?

   **APPLY:** (question 30, p. 127) How has a past difficult circumstance taught you joy and strengthened your faith?

**5. WRAP-UP:** (p. 127) What aspect of God's character has this week's passage of Hebrews shown you more clearly?

Fill in the following statement:

Knowing that God is _____ shows me that I am _____.

What one step can you take this week to better live in light of this truth?

## WEEK EIGHT | VIEWER GUIDE NOTES

Teaching sessions available
for purchase or rent at
LifeWay.com/Better

WEEK EIGHT: BETTER SACRIFICE     131

# Week Nine:

## Consider the Faithful

Remember to take time this week to read repetitively. Spend some time committing the passage you chose to memory. Try reciting it aloud to someone.

This week we will walk through the famous "Hall of Faith" of Hebrews 11. You'll be asked to look back to the Old Testament to trace how these names came to be found here. It may be a little time-consuming, but do your best to read and savor each of the stories, reflecting on how they add weight to the faithfulness of the person described and the faithfulness of the God they all served. You will have fewer questions this week to allow you time to draw connections. To its original audience, this chapter would have needed no review session, so familiar were they with the names it includes. My hope is that our study efforts this week will help move us closer to their perspective by calling to mind the stories of familiar names and exploring those of the less familiar.

**READ THIS WEEK'S PASSAGE: HEBREWS 11:1-40.**

1. In 2–3 sentences summarize the main ideas of the passage.

2. What "better than" comparisons are made in this week's passage?

3. Continue your annotating as in previous weeks:
   - Mark *therefore* and any synonyms for it in your copy of the text with **a purple capital T and underline**.
   - Mark every occurrence of the word *better* in this week's section of the text with **a yellow highlighter**.
   - Mark every occurrence of the word *perfect* or *perfection* with **an orange P and underline**.
   - Mark every occurrence of the word *faithful* or *faith* with **a wiggly green underline**.

4. How does this week's section of the text follow logically from the previous one?

**NOW LOOK MORE CLOSELY AT HEBREWS 11:1-7.**

5.  In 11:1-3 the author began with a summary statement about the nature of faith. How did he define faith (11:1)?

    " ... the _____ of things _____,

    the _____ of things _____."

    What role did he say faith played in the lives of "the people of old" (11:2)?

    How does 11:3 further explain 11:1?

6.  Look up 2 Corinthians 4:16-18. How does its message reinforce the picture of faith in Hebrews 11:1-3?

7.  Next to each reference on the left below, note the subject (who did what) of each "by faith" statement in 11:1-7. Then look up the passages in the column to the right. Draw a line to connect each subject to the passage in which his story is found.

    11:3—By faith, *we understand that the universe was created by the word of God.*                Genesis 5:18-24

    11:4—By faith,                                                                                   Genesis 6:9-14

    11:5—By faith,                                                                                   Genesis 4:1-10

    11:7—By faith,                                                                                   Genesis 1:1

What do you notice about the way the author of Hebrews was unfolding his story of faith? How is it an orderly account?

8. What two requirements does 11:6 give for those who would draw near to God? List them below and note why each is important.

    1.

    2.

9. How would 11:6 answer someone who claimed we can do nothing to please God?

10. APPLY: Abel's faith showed itself in a generous offering. Enoch's faith showed itself in a steady walk of obedience. Noah's faith showed itself in a reverent fear of God that overrode his fear of man's opinion. Which of these faithful people that we have met so far would you most like to emulate? Why?

**NOW LOOK AT HEBREWS 11:8-22.**

11. Hebrews 11:1-7 covers what is known as the "primordial history" of the Book of Genesis (Gen. 1–11). In 11:8-22 the author covers the "patriarchal history" of Genesis (Gen. 12–50) because it traces the stories of the patriarchs—Abraham, Isaac, Jacob, and Joseph. Next to each reference on the left below, note the subject of each "by faith" statement in 11:8-22. Then look up the passages in the column to the right. Draw a line to connect each person to the passage in which his or her story is found.

| | |
|---|---|
| 11:8-9—By faith, | Genesis 48:1-21 |
| 11:11—By faith, | Genesis 12:1-9 |
| 11:17—By faith, | Genesis 22:1-19 |
| 11:20—By faith, | Genesis 21:1-7 |
| 11:21—By faith, | Genesis 50:24-26 |
| 11:22—By faith, | Genesis 27:1-40 |

12. On which person does the text spend most of its time?

In your opinion, what part of his story most illustrates his faithfulness? Why?

13. What attitude did Abraham have toward his life on earth? How do you think he would have defined *home*? List every evidence from 11:8-16 you can find.

14. Abraham, Isaac, and Jacob lived as strangers and exiles who desired "a better country" (11:16). How would their examples have been both reassuring and convicting to the author's original audience?

15. **APPLY:** How should the examples of Abraham, Isaac, and Jacob living as strangers and exiles who desired "a better country" be both reassuring and convicting to you?

**NOW LOOK AT HEBREWS 11:23-31.**

16. Continuing his walk through the Old Testament, the author found more examples of faith in Exodus and Joshua. Next to each reference on the left below, note the subject of each "by faith" statement in 11:23-31. Then look up the passages in the column to the right. Draw a line to connect each subject to the passage in which his or her story is found.

    11:23—By faith,                              Joshua 6:1-21

    11:24-26—By faith,                           Exodus 14:1-30

    11:27-28—By faith,                           Exodus 2:1-2

    11:29—By faith,                              Exodus 4:18-20

    11:30—By faith,                              Joshua 6:22-25

    11:31—By faith,                              Exodus 12:21-32

17. Choose one of the faithful people in this passage, and list out every fear you think they likely would have faced.

18. What is the proper relationship between fear and faith, based on the example of the person you chose above?

19. **APPLY:** What specific fears are you currently facing? How do you think the people mentioned in Hebrews 11 would encourage you to respond to them?

**NOW LOOK AT HEBREWS 11:32-40.**

20. How do the names mentioned in 11:32 continue the author's walk through the Old Testament? In what books are their stories found?

21. How would this passage answer someone who claimed that God grants a life of ease to those who are faithful?

22. Read 11:39-40 aloud, emphasizing *us* and *they* as you read. Then rewrite these verses in your own words, getting as close to the author's meaning as you are able, in light of all we have seen in this chapter.

23. **APPLY:** What faithful person have you known whom you would describe as someone "of whom the world was not worthy" (11:38)? What one aspect of Christlikeness in him or her stands out to you the most? What step can you take to imitate it?

## WRAP-UP

What aspect of God's character has this week's passage of Hebrews shown you more clearly?

Fill in the following statement:

Knowing that God is _____ shows me that
I am _____.

What one step can you take this week to better live in light of this truth?

**INTRODUCTORY QUESTION:** Do you know your ethnic background? Where are your ancestors from?

1. **OBSERVE:** (question 9, p. 136) How would 11:6 answer someone who claimed we can do nothing to please God?

   **APPLY:** (question 10, p. 136) Abel's faith showed itself in a generous offering. Enoch's faith showed itself in a steady walk of obedience. Noah's faith showed itself in a reverent fear of God that overrode his fear of man's opinion. Which of these faithful people that we have met so far would you most like to emulate? Why?

2. **OBSERVE:** (question 14, p. 138) Abraham, Isaac, and Jacob lived as strangers and exiles who desired "a better country" (11:16). How would their examples have been both reassuring and convicting to the author's original audience?

   **APPLY:** (question 15, p. 138) How should the examples of Abraham, Isaac, and Jacob living as strangers and exiles who desired "a better country" be both reassuring and convicting to you?

3. **OBSERVE:** (question 18, p. 139) What is the proper relationship between fear and faith, based on the example of the person you chose in question 17?

   **APPLY:** (question 19, p. 139) What specific fears are you currently facing? How do you think the people mentioned in Hebrews 11 would encourage you to respond to them?

4. **OBSERVE:** (question 21, p. 140) How would this passage answer someone who claimed that God grants a life of ease to those who are faithful?

**APPLY:** (question 23, p. 140) What faithful person have you known whom you would describe as someone "of whom the world was not worthy" (11:38)? What one aspect of Christlikeness in him or her stands out to you the most? What step can you take to imitate it?

5. **WRAP-UP:** (p. 141) What aspect of God's character has this week's passage of Hebrews shown you more clearly?

Fill in the following statement:

Knowing that God is _____ shows me that
I am _____.

What one step can you take this week to better live in light of this truth?

## WEEK NINE | VIEWER GUIDE NOTES

# Week Ten:

## Run the Race

Having placed before us an array of the faithful who set aside their fears to walk forward in obedience, the author of Hebrews would then exhort us to their examples. He encouraged endurance in the face of opposition, reminding us that our heavenly Father's discipline of His children is always benevolent. The author lifted our eyes to a vision of joy-laden Mount Zion, the dwelling place of our God, ablaze with glory. As he closed out his letter, he took care to point his readers toward the implications of his arguments. How should the recognition that Jesus is better spur them in their daily lives to run the race and offer acceptable worship to God?

## DAY ONE

### READ THIS WEEK'S PASSAGE: HEBREWS 12:1–13:25.

1.  In 2–3 sentences summarize the main ideas of the passage.

2.  What "better than" comparisons are made in this week's passage?

3.  Continue your annotating as in previous weeks:
    - ☐ Mark the words *covenant* and *Moses* in this week's section of the text with **a red C or M**.
    - ☐ Mark *therefore* and any synonyms for it in your copy of the text with **a purple capital T and underline**.
    - ☐ Mark every occurrence of the word *better* in this week's section of the text with **a yellow highlighter**.
    - ☐ Mark every occurrence of the word *perfect*, *perfection*, or *perfector* with **an orange P and underline**.
    - ☐ Mark every occurrence of *a familial term* (sons, brothers, children) with **a blue underline**.
    - ☐ Mark every occurrence of the word *faithful* or *faith* with **a wiggly green underline**.

4.  How does this week's section of the text follow logically from the previous one? What previous idea is the *therefore* in 12:1 building on? Summarize it below.

## NOW LOOK MORE CLOSELY AT HEBREWS 12:1-11.

5.   What two exhortations are we given in 12:1? How do they relate to one another?

6.   The author introduced the metaphor of a runner in a race to illustrate the nature of the Christian life. How is this an accurate and helpful picture?

7.   What dual role is Jesus described as fulfilling in 12:2? Why are each of these roles important?

8.   The virtue of endurance is offered to us as a necessary part of running our races. Mark each occurrence of the word *endurance* or *endure(d)* in 12:1-11 with a brown E. Draw an arrow back to those whose endurance is being highlighted. Then fill in the following statement:

     _____ should endure because _____ endured.

9.   In 12:5-7 the author connected the virtue of discipline to the call to endure, quoting Proverbs 3:11-12. In 12:5-11, mark every occurrence of the word *discipline* with a black D. How many times does it occur in these seven verses?

10. What human relationship did the author use to explain the discipline of God? How is it helpful?

11. **APPLY:** How have you experienced the discipline of the Lord? How has it trained you away from sin and toward holiness? What "peaceful fruit of righteousness" has it borne in your life (12:11)?

## DAY THREE

**NOW LOOK AT HEBREWS 12:12-29.**

12. What previous idea is the *therefore* in 12:12 building on? Summarize it below.

13. How does the admonition of 12:14 point back to the assurance of 12:11?

14. What three things are we told to "see to" in 12:15-16?

    1.

    2.

    3.

15. Esau is presented to us as a negative example in 12:16-17. Look back at his story in Genesis 25:29-34. What specific sinful attitudes cause him to be listed here in Hebrews as "unholy"?

    How was Esau's light regard for what was of true value a timely example for the original hearers of Hebrews to consider?

16. What two contrasting images are presented in 12:18-24? Write them below and then note how each is described. Then choose one adjective that you think would best describe each of them.

| MOUNT _____ (SEE ALSO EXODUS 19:1-25.) | MOUNT _____ |
| --- | --- |
| | |

17. We looked at Abel's story briefly last week (11:4). Now we see his shed blood compared to Christ's (12:24). In what sense does the sprinkled blood of Christ speak "a better word than the blood of Abel"? Give your best answer.

Abel's "word":


Christ's "word":


18. What warning did the author give, in light of his discussion of "how it used to be" and "how it is or will be" (12:25)?


Is this warning directed at believers or at unbelievers? Explain your answer.

19. The author quoted Haggai 2:6, a prophecy about Christ's second coming. According to 12:26-27, what can be shaken? What cannot be shaken? Summarize the author's point in one sentence.

20. According to 12:28-29, what is the proper response to understanding that the God of Mount Zion will one day judge heaven and earth?

    12:28a—" ... let us

    12:28b—" ... let us

21. Look up the words *reverence* and *awe* in a dictionary or thesaurus and write a definition for them below, one that fits with the context of Hebrews 12:28.
    REVERENCE:

    AWE:

    Based on your definitions above, how would you describe worship that is "unacceptable"?

22. APPLY: Think about our modern conceptions of what constitutes "acceptable worship." How closely do they fit the description of Hebrews 12:28-29? How might these expressions look different if they had as their reference point "our God is a consuming fire" (12:29)?

**NOW LOOK AT HEBREWS 13:1-16.**

23. An admonition is given in 13:1 that sets the tone for those that will follow in the next five verses. What is it? (Note: the word *brotherly* means *brother-sisterly*, connoting sibling affection between two people.)

Paraphrase each of the four admonitions that follow. Then note how submitting to the command you wrote above would help you submit to each of them.

13:2

13:3

13:4

13:5

24. In discussing the love of money in 13:5-6 the author quotes Deuteronomy 31:6 and Psalm 118:6. What do these two quotations point toward as the underlying fears behind the love of money?

25. What do you think is the relationship between the admonition in 13:7 and the statement in 13:8?

26. What do you think is the author's point in 13:9-10? Look up Deuteronomy 18:1 to help your understanding.

27. Under the old covenant, various types of offerings were made for various reasons. As we saw above, certain types or parts of offerings were eaten. The "sin offering," however, was never eaten, but was instead taken and burned outside the camp. Look up Mark 15:20-22, and note how Jesus' death followed the pattern of the sin offering.

28. Immediately after the *therefore* in 13:13, the author named three pleasing sacrifices his hearers could offer to God. Write them below in your own words.

    **13:13**

    **13:15**

    **13:16**

29. **APPLY:** Which of the four admonitions in 13:2-5 most needs your attention? Write it below. Which brother or sister would know your love for them more deeply if you were to make a greater effort to obey it?

**NOW LOOK AT HEBREWS 13:17-25.**

30. What three requests did the author make with regard to how we should relate to our leaders (13:17-19)?

    1.

    2.

    3.

    Which did he seem to regard as the most urgent request? Explain your answer.

31. How is God described in the beautiful benediction of 13:20-21? Who is He? What has He done? What will He do?

    How is Jesus described?

32. All Scripture is "breathed out by God and profitable" (2 Tim. 3:16). What profit can you take from the final greetings of 13:22-25? List a few thoughts below.

33. **APPLY:** How do modern-day church members make it difficult for their leaders to lead? How would applying the overarching principle of brotherly and sisterly love to our relationships with those who lead us affect the way we follow their lead?

## WRAP-UP

What aspect of God's character has this week's passage of Hebrews shown you more clearly?

Fill in the following statement:

Knowing that God is _____ shows me that
I am _____.

What one step can you take this week to better live in light of this truth?

**INTRODUCTORY QUESTION:** Would you rather spend your vacation in the mountains or on the beach?

1. **OBSERVE:** (question 10, p. 150) What human relationship did the author use to explain the discipline of God? How is it helpful?

   **APPLY:** (question 11, p. 150) How have you experienced the discipline of the Lord? How has it trained you away from sin and toward holiness? What "peaceful fruit of righteousness" has it borne in your life (12:11)?

2. **OBSERVE:** (question 21, p. 153) Based on your definitions of *reverence* and *awe*, how would you describe worship that is "unacceptable"?

   **APPLY:** (question 22, p. 153) Think about our modern conceptions of what constitutes "acceptable worship." How closely do they fit the description of Hebrews 12:28-29? How might these expressions look different if they had as their reference point "our God is a consuming fire" (12:29)?

3. **OBSERVE:** (question 23, p. 154) An admonition is given in 13:1 that sets the tone for those that will follow in the next five verses. What is it? (Note: the word *brotherly* means *brother-sisterly*, connoting sibling affection between two people.)

   **APPLY:** (question 29, p. 155) Which of the four admonitions in 13:2-5 most needs your attention? Write it below. Which brother or sister would know your love for them more deeply if you were to make a greater effort to obey it?

4. **OBSERVE:** (question 30, p. 156) What three requests did the author make with regard to how we should relate to our leaders (13:17-19)? Which did he seem to regard as the most urgent request? Explain your answer.

**APPLY:** (question 33, p. 157) How do modern-day church members make it difficult for their leaders to lead? How would applying the overarching principle of brotherly and sisterly love to our relationships with those who lead us affect the way we follow their lead?

5. **WRAP-UP:** (p. 157) What aspect of God's character has this week's passage of Hebrews shown you more clearly?

Fill in the following statement:
Knowing that God is _____ shows me that
I am _____.

What one step can you take this week to better live in light of this truth?

## WEEK TEN | VIEWER GUIDE NOTES

Teaching sessions available
for purchase or rent at
LifeWay.com/Better

WEEK TEN: RUN THE RACE          161

# Wrap-up

You did it! You faithfully walked through the text of Hebrews, learning from both the Old and New Testament stories of faithfulness. Now it's time to reflect on what you've learned, taking comprehension, interpretation, and application out into the world.

Here is an optional wrap-up session to help you process what you've learned and live out the message of a better promise, a better hope, a better covenant, and a better plan.

**READ STRAIGHT THROUGH THE BOOK OF HEBREWS.**

As you read, think back on what you've learned throughout your study. Answer the following questions.

1. What attribute of God—as revealed in Jesus Christ—has emerged most clearly as you have studied this letter?

How does knowing this truth about Him change the way you see yourself?

How should knowing this truth change the way you live?

2.  How has the Holy Spirit used Hebrews to convict you of sin? What thoughts, words, or actions has He shown you that need to be redeemed? What do you need to stop doing?

3.  How has the Holy Spirit used Hebrews to train you in righteousness? What disciplines has He given you a desire to pursue? What do you need to start doing?

4. How has the Holy Spirit used Hebrews to encourage you? What cause to celebrate has this letter imprinted on your heart?

5. What verse or passage from Hebrews stands out most in your mind after ten weeks of study? Why?

Close in prayer. Pray through the benediction of 13:20-21:

*O God of peace who brought again from the dead my Lord Jesus, the Great Shepherd of the sheep, by the blood of the eternal covenant, equip me with everything good that I may do Your will, working in me that which is pleasing in Your sight, through Jesus Christ, to whom be glory forever and ever. Amen.*

### THE SUPREMACY OF GOD'S SON

[1]Long ago, at many times and in many ways, God spoke to our fathers by the prophets, [2]but in these last days he has spoken to us by his Son, whom he appointed the heir of all things, through whom also he created the world. [3]He is the radiance of the glory of God and the exact imprint of his nature, and he upholds the universe by the word of his power. After making purification for sins, he sat down at the right hand of the Majesty on high, [4]having become as much superior to angels as the name he has inherited is more excellent than theirs.

[5]For to which of the angels did God ever say,

"You are my Son,
     today I have begotten you"?

Or again,

"I will be to him a father,
     and he shall be to me a son"?

[6]And again, when he brings the firstborn into the world, he says,

"Let all God's angels worship him."

[7]Of the angels he says,

"He makes his angels winds,
     and his ministers a flame of fire."

[8]But of the Son he says,

"Your throne, O God, is forever and ever,
     the scepter of uprightness is the scepter of your kingdom.
[9]You have loved righteousness and hated wickedness;
therefore God, your God, has anointed you
     with the oil of gladness beyond your companions."

[10]And,

"You, Lord, laid the foundation of the earth in the beginning,
     and the heavens are the work of your hands;

<sup>11</sup>they will perish, but you remain;

    they will all wear out like a garment,

<sup>12</sup>like a robe you will roll them up,

    like a garment they will be changed.

But you are the same,

    and your years will have no end."

<sup>13</sup>And to which of the angels has he ever said,

"Sit at my right hand

    until I make your enemies a footstool for your feet"?

<sup>14</sup>Are they not all ministering spirits sent out to serve for the sake of those who are to inherit salvation?

## HEBREWS 2

### WARNING AGAINST NEGLECTING SALVATION

Therefore we must pay much closer attention to what we have heard, lest we drift away from it. <sup>2</sup>For since the message declared by angels proved to be reliable, and every transgression or disobedience received a just retribution, <sup>3</sup>how shall we escape if we neglect such a great salvation? It was declared at first by the Lord, and it was attested to us by those who heard, <sup>4</sup>while God also bore witness by signs and wonders and various miracles and by gifts of the Holy Spirit distributed according to his will.

### THE FOUNDER OF SALVATION

<sup>5</sup>For it was not to angels that God subjected the world to come, of which we are speaking. <sup>6</sup>It has been testified somewhere,

"What is man, that you are mindful of him,

    or the son of man, that you care for him?

<sup>7</sup>You made him for a little while lower than the angels;

you have crowned him with glory and honor,

 [8] putting everything in subjection under his feet."

Now in putting everything in subjection to him, he left nothing outside his control. At present, we do not yet see everything in subjection to him. [9]But we see him who for a little while was made lower than the angels, namely Jesus, crowned with glory and honor because of the suffering of death, so that by the grace of God he might taste death for everyone.

[10]For it was fitting that he, for whom and by whom all things exist, in bringing many sons to glory, should make the founder of their salvation perfect through suffering. [11]For he who sanctifies and those who are sanctified all have one source. That is why he is not ashamed to call them brothers, [12]saying,

"I will tell of your name to my brothers;

 in the midst of the congregation I will sing your praise."

[13]And again,

"I will put my trust in him."

And again,

"Behold, I and the children God has given me."

[14]Since therefore the children share in flesh and blood, he himself likewise partook of the same things, that through death he might destroy the one who has the power of death, that is, the devil, [15]and deliver all those who through fear of death were subject to lifelong slavery. [16]For surely it is not angels that he helps, but he helps the offspring of Abraham. [17]Therefore he had to be made like his brothers in every respect, so that he might become a merciful and faithful high priest in the service of God, to make propitiation for the sins of the people. [18]For because he himself has suffered when tempted, he is able to help those who are being tempted.

### JESUS GREATER THAN MOSES

Therefore, holy brothers, you who share in a heavenly calling, consider Jesus, the apostle and high priest of our confession, [2]who was faithful to him who appointed him, just as Moses also was faithful in all God's house. [3]For Jesus has been counted worthy of more glory than Moses—as much more glory as the builder of a house has more honor than the house itself. [4](For every house is built by someone, but the builder of all things is God.) [5]Now Moses was faithful in all God's house as a servant, to testify to the things that were to be spoken later, [6]but Christ is faithful over God's house as a son. And we are his house, if indeed we hold fast our confidence and our boasting in our hope.

### A REST FOR THE PEOPLE OF GOD

[7]Therefore, as the Holy Spirit says,

"Today, if you hear his voice,
[8]do not harden your hearts as in the rebellion,
   on the day of testing in the wilderness,
[9]where your fathers put me to the test
   and saw my works for forty years.
[10]Therefore I was provoked with that generation,
and said, 'They always go astray in their heart;
   they have not known my ways.'
[11]As I swore in my wrath,
   'They shall not enter my rest.'"

[12]Take care, brothers, lest there be in any of you an evil, unbelieving heart, leading you to fall away from the living God. [13]But exhort one another every day, as long as it is called "today," that none of you may be hardened by the deceitfulness of sin. [14]For we have come to share in Christ, if indeed we hold our original confidence firm to the end. [15]As it is said,

"Today, if you hear his voice,

do not harden your hearts as in the rebellion."

[16] For who were those who heard and yet rebelled? Was it not all those who left Egypt led by Moses? [17] And with whom was he provoked for forty years? Was it not with those who sinned, whose bodies fell in the wilderness? [18] And to whom did he swear that they would not enter his rest, but to those who were disobedient? [19] So we see that they were unable to enter because of unbelief.

## HEBREWS 4

Therefore, while the promise of entering his rest still stands, let us fear lest any of you should seem to have failed to reach it. [2] For good news came to us just as to them, but the message they heard did not benefit them, because they were not united by faith with those who listened. [3] For we who have believed enter that rest, as he has said,

"As I swore in my wrath,

'They shall not enter my rest,'"

although his works were finished from the foundation of the world. [4] For he has somewhere spoken of the seventh day in this way: "And God rested on the seventh day from all his works." [5] And again in this passage he said,

"They shall not enter my rest."

[6] Since therefore it remains for some to enter it, and those who formerly received the good news failed to enter because of disobedience, [7] again he appoints a certain day, "Today," saying through David so long afterward, in the words already quoted,

"Today, if you hear his voice,

do not harden your hearts."

[8] For if Joshua had given them rest, God would not have spoken of another day later on. [9] So then, there remains a Sabbath rest for the people of God,

[10]for whoever has entered God's rest has also rested from his works as God did from his.

[11]Let us therefore strive to enter that rest, so that no one may fall by the same sort of disobedience. [12]For the word of God is living and active, sharper than any two-edged sword, piercing to the division of soul and of spirit, of joints and of marrow, and discerning the thoughts and intentions of the heart. [13]And no creature is hidden from his sight, but all are naked and exposed to the eyes of him to whom we must give account.

## JESUS THE GREAT HIGH PRIEST

[14]Since then we have a great high priest who has passed through the heavens, Jesus, the Son of God, let us hold fast our confession. [15]For we do not have a high priest who is unable to sympathize with our weaknesses, but one who in every respect has been tempted as we are, yet without sin. [16]Let us then with confidence draw near to the throne of grace, that we may receive mercy and find grace to help in time of need.

## HEBREWS 5

For every high priest chosen from among men is appointed to act on behalf of men in relation to God, to offer gifts and sacrifices for sins. [2]He can deal gently with the ignorant and wayward, since he himself is beset with weakness. [3]Because of this he is obligated to offer sacrifice for his own sins just as he does for those of the people. [4]And no one takes this honor for himself, but only when called by God, just as Aaron was. [5]So also Christ did not exalt himself to be made a high priest, but was appointed by him who said to him,

"You are my Son,
    today I have begotten you";
[6]as he says also in another place,

"You are a priest forever,

> after the order of Melchizedek."

[7] In the days of his flesh, Jesus offered up prayers and supplications, with loud cries and tears, to him who was able to save him from death, and he was heard because of his reverence. [8] Although he was a son, he learned obedience through what he suffered. [9] And being made perfect, he became the source of eternal salvation to all who obey him, [10] being designated by God a high priest after the order of Melchizedek.

## WARNING AGAINST APOSTASY

[11] About this we have much to say, and it is hard to explain, since you have become dull of hearing. [12] For though by this time you ought to be teachers, you need someone to teach you again the basic principles of the oracles of God. You need milk, not solid food, [13] for everyone who lives on milk is unskilled in the word of righteousness, since he is a child. [14] But solid food is for the mature, for those who have their powers of discernment trained by constant practice to distinguish good from evil.

## HEBREWS 6

Therefore let us leave the elementary doctrine of Christ and go on to maturity, not laying again a foundation of repentance from dead works and of faith toward God, [2] and of instruction about washings, the laying on of hands, the resurrection of the dead, and eternal judgment. [3] And this we will do if God permits. [4] For it is impossible, in the case of those who have once been enlightened, who have tasted the heavenly gift, and have shared in the Holy Spirit, [5] and have tasted the goodness of the word of God and the powers of the age to come, [6] and then have fallen away, to restore them again to repentance, since they are crucifying once again the Son of God to their own harm and holding him up to contempt. [7] For land that has drunk the rain that often falls on it, and produces a crop useful to those for whose sake it is cultivated, receives a blessing from God. [8]But if it bears thorns and thistles, it is worthless and near to being cursed, and its end is to be burned. [9]Though we speak in this way, yet in your case, beloved, we feel sure of better things—things that belong to salvation. [10]For God is not unjust so as to overlook your work and the love that you have shown for his name in serving the saints, as you still do. [11]And we desire each one of you to show the same earnestness to have the full assurance of hope until the end, [12]so that you may not be sluggish, but imitators of those who through faith and patience inherit the promises.

## THE CERTAINTY OF GOD'S PROMISE

[13]For when God made a promise to Abraham, since he had no one greater by whom to swear, he swore by himself, [14]saying, "Surely I will bless you and multiply you." [15]And thus Abraham, having patiently waited, obtained the promise. [16]For people swear by something greater than themselves, and in all their disputes an oath is final for confirmation. [17]So when God desired to show more convincingly to the heirs of the promise the unchangeable character of his purpose, he guaranteed it with an oath, [18]so that by two unchangeable things, in which it is impossible for God to lie, we who have fled for refuge might have strong encouragement to hold fast to the hope set before us. [19]We have this as a sure and steadfast anchor of the soul, a hope that enters into the inner place behind the curtain, [20]where Jesus has gone as a forerunner on our behalf, having become a high priest forever after the order of Melchizedek.

## HEBREWS 7

## THE PRIESTLY ORDER OF MELCHIZEDEK

For this Melchizedek, king of Salem, priest of the Most High God, met Abraham returning from the slaughter of the kings and blessed him, [2]and to him Abraham apportioned a tenth part of everything. He is first, by translation of his name, king of righteousness, and then he is also king of Salem, that is, king of peace. [3] He is without father or mother or genealogy, having neither beginning of days nor end of life, but resembling the Son of God he continues a priest forever.

[4] See how great this man was to whom Abraham the patriarch gave a tenth of the spoils! [5] And those descendants of Levi who receive the priestly office have a commandment in the law to take tithes from the people, that is, from their brothers, though these also are descended from Abraham. [6] But this man who does not have his descent from them received tithes from Abraham and blessed him who had the promises. [7] It is beyond dispute that the inferior is blessed by the superior. [8] In the one case tithes are received by mortal men, but in the other case, by one of whom it is testified that he lives. [9] One might even say that Levi himself, who receives tithes, paid tithes through Abraham, [10] for he was still in the loins of his ancestor when Melchizedek met him.

## JESUS COMPARED TO MELCHIZEDEK

[11] Now if perfection had been attainable through the Levitical priesthood (for under it the people received the law), what further need would there have been for another priest to arise after the order of Melchizedek, rather than one named after the order of Aaron? [12] For when there is a change in the priesthood, there is necessarily a change in the law as well. [13] For the one of whom these things are spoken belonged to another tribe, from which no one has ever served at the altar. [14] For it is evident that our Lord was descended from Judah, and in connection with that tribe Moses said nothing about priests.

[15] This becomes even more evident when another priest arises in the likeness of Melchizedek, [16] who has become a priest, not on the basis of a legal requirement concerning bodily descent, but by the power of an indestructible life. [17] For it is witnessed of him,

"You are a priest forever,

    after the order of Melchizedek."

[18]For on the one hand, a former commandment is set aside because of its weakness and uselessness [19](for the law made nothing perfect); but on the other hand, a better hope is introduced, through which we draw near to God.

[20]And it was not without an oath. For those who formerly became priests were made such without an oath, [21]but this one was made a priest with an oath by the one who said to him:

"The Lord has sworn

    and will not change his mind,

'You are a priest forever.'"

[22]This makes Jesus the guarantor of a better covenant.

[23]The former priests were many in number, because they were prevented by death from continuing in office, [24]but he holds his priesthood permanently, because he continues forever. [25]Consequently, he is able to save to the uttermost those who draw near to God through him, since he always lives to make intercession for them.

[26]For it was indeed fitting that we should have such a high priest, holy, innocent, unstained, separated from sinners, and exalted above the heavens. [27]He has no need, like those high priests, to offer sacrifices daily, first for his own sins and then for those of the people, since he did this once for all when he offered up himself. [28]For the law appoints men in their weakness as high priests, but the word of the oath, which came later than the law, appoints a Son who has been made perfect forever.

## JESUS, HIGH PRIEST OF A BETTER COVENANT

Now the point in what we are saying is this: we have such a high priest, one who is seated at the right hand of the throne of the Majesty in heaven, [2]a minister in the holy places, in the true tent that the Lord set up, not man. [3]For every high priest is appointed to offer gifts and sacrifices; thus it is necessary for this priest also to have something to offer. [4]Now if he were on earth, he would not be a priest at all, since there are priests who offer gifts according to the law. [5]They serve a copy and shadow of the heavenly things. For when Moses was about to erect the tent, he was instructed by God, saying, "See that you make everything according to the pattern that was shown you on the mountain." [6]But as it is, Christ has obtained a ministry that is as much more excellent than the old as the covenant he mediates is better, since it is enacted on better promises. [7]For if that first covenant had been faultless, there would have been no occasion to look for a second.

[8]For he finds fault with them when he says:

"Behold, the days are coming, declares the Lord,

>     when I will establish a new covenant with the house of Israel
>     and with the house of Judah,

[9]not like the covenant that I made with their fathers

>     on the day when I took them by the hand to bring them out of the land
>     of Egypt.

For they did not continue in my covenant,

>     and so I showed no concern for them, declares the Lord.

[10]For this is the covenant that I will make with the house of Israel

>     after those days, declares the Lord:

I will put my laws into their minds,

>     and write them on their hearts,

and I will be their God,

and they shall be my people.

[11] And they shall not teach, each one his neighbor
and each one his brother, saying, 'Know the Lord,'
for they shall all know me,
from the least of them to the greatest.

[12] For I will be merciful toward their iniquities,
and I will remember their sins no more."

[13] In speaking of a new covenant, he makes the first one obsolete. And what is becoming obsolete and growing old is ready to vanish away.

## HEBREWS 9

### THE EARTHLY HOLY PLACE

Now even the first covenant had regulations for worship and an earthly place of holiness. [2] For a tent was prepared, the first section, in which were the lampstand and the table and the bread of the Presence. It is called the Holy Place. [3] Behind the second curtain was a second section called the Most Holy Place, [4] having the golden altar of incense and the ark of the covenant covered on all sides with gold, in which was a golden urn holding the manna, and Aaron's staff that budded, and the tablets of the covenant. [5] Above it were the cherubim of glory overshadowing the mercy seat. Of these things we cannot now speak in detail.

[6] These preparations having thus been made, the priests go regularly into the first section, performing their ritual duties, [7] but into the second only the high priest goes, and he but once a year, and not without taking blood, which he offers for himself and for the unintentional sins of the people. [8] By this the Holy Spirit indicates that the way into the holy places is not yet opened as long as the first section is still standing [9] (which is symbolic for the present age). According to this arrangement, gifts and sacrifices are offered that cannot perfect the conscience of the worshiper, [10] but deal

only with food and drink and various washings, regulations for the body imposed until the time of reformation.

## REDEMPTION THROUGH THE BLOOD OF CHRIST

[11]But when Christ appeared as a high priest of the good things that have come, then through the greater and more perfect tent (not made with hands, that is, not of this creation) [12]he entered once for all into the holy places, not by means of the blood of goats and calves but by means of his own blood, thus securing an eternal redemption. [13]For if the blood of goats and bulls, and the sprinkling of defiled persons with the ashes of a heifer, sanctify for the purification of the flesh, [14]how much more will the blood of Christ, who through the eternal Spirit offered himself without blemish to God, purify our conscience from dead works to serve the living God. [15]Therefore he is the mediator of a new covenant, so that those who are called may receive the promised eternal inheritance, since a death has occurred that redeems them from the transgressions committed under the first covenant. [16]For where a will is involved, the death of the one who made it must be established. [17]For a will takes effect only at death, since it is not in force as long as the one who made it is alive. [18]Therefore not even the first covenant was inaugurated without blood. [19]For when every commandment of the law had been declared by Moses to all the people, he took the blood of calves and goats, with water and scarlet wool and hyssop, and sprinkled both the book itself and all the people, [20]saying, "This is the blood of the covenant that God commanded for you." [21]And in the same way he sprinkled with the blood both the tent and all the vessels used in worship. [22]Indeed, under the law almost everything is purified with blood, and without the shedding of blood there is no forgiveness of sins. [23]Thus it was necessary for the copies of the heavenly things to be purified with these rites, but the heavenly things themselves with better sacrifices than these. [24]For Christ has entered, not into holy places made with hands,

which are copies of the true things, but into heaven itself, now to appear in the presence of God on our behalf. [25] Nor was it to offer himself repeatedly, as the high priest enters the holy places every year with blood not his own, [26] for then he would have had to suffer repeatedly since the foundation of the world. But as it is, he has appeared once for all at the end of the ages to put away sin by the sacrifice of himself. [27] And just as it is appointed for man to die once, and after that comes judgment, [28] so Christ, having been offered once to bear the sins of many, will appear a second time, not to deal with sin but to save those who are eagerly waiting for him.

## HEBREWS 10

### CHRIST'S SACRIFICE ONCE FOR ALL

For since the law has but a shadow of the good things to come instead of the true form of these realities, it can never, by the same sacrifices that are continually offered every year, make perfect those who draw near. [2] Otherwise, would they not have ceased to be offered, since the worshipers, having once been cleansed, would no longer have any consciousness of sins? [3] But in these sacrifices there is a reminder of sins every year. [4] For it is impossible for the blood of bulls and goats to take away sins. [5] Consequently, when Christ came into the world, he said,

"Sacrifices and offerings you have not desired,
    but a body have you prepared for me;
[6] in burnt offerings and sin offerings
    you have taken no pleasure.
[7] Then I said, 'Behold, I have come to do your will, O God,
    as it is written of me in the scroll of the book.'"

[8] When he said above, "You have neither desired nor taken pleasure in sacrifices and offerings and burnt offerings and sin offerings" (these are offered according to the law), [9] then he added, "Behold, I have come to do

your will." He does away with the first in order to establish the second. [10]And by that will we have been sanctified through the offering of the body of Jesus Christ once for all.

[11]And every priest stands daily at his service, offering repeatedly the same sacrifices, which can never take away sins. [12]But when Christ had offered for all time a single sacrifice for sins, he sat down at the right hand of God, [13]waiting from that time until his enemies should be made a footstool for his feet. [14]For by a single offering he has perfected for all time those who are being sanctified.

[15]And the Holy Spirit also bears witness to us; for after saying,

[16]"This is the covenant that I will make with them
   after those days, declares the Lord:
I will put my laws on their hearts,
   and write them on their minds,"

[17]then he adds,

"I will remember their sins and their lawless deeds no more."

[18]Where there is forgiveness of these, there is no longer any offering for sin.

## THE FULL ASSURANCE OF FAITH

[19]Therefore, brothers, since we have confidence to enter the holy places by the blood of Jesus, [20]by the new and living way that he opened for us through the curtain, that is, through his flesh, [21]and since we have a great priest over the house of God, [22]let us draw near with a true heart in full assurance of faith, with our hearts sprinkled clean from an evil conscience and our bodies washed with pure water. [23]Let us hold fast the confession of our hope without wavering, for he who promised is faithful. [24]And let us consider how to stir up one another to love and good works, [25]not neglecting to meet together, as is the habit of some, but encouraging one another, and all the more as you see the Day drawing near.

[26]For if we go on sinning deliberately after receiving the knowledge of the truth, there no longer remains a sacrifice for sins, [27]but a fearful

expectation of judgment, and a fury of fire that will consume the adversaries. [28] Anyone who has set aside the law of Moses dies without mercy on the evidence of two or three witnesses. [29] How much worse punishment, do you think, will be deserved by the one who has trampled underfoot the Son of God, and has profaned the blood of the covenant by which he was sanctified, and has outraged the Spirit of grace? [30] For we know him who said, "Vengeance is mine; I will repay." And again, "The Lord will judge his people." [31] It is a fearful thing to fall into the hands of the living God.

[32] But recall the former days when, after you were enlightened, you endured a hard struggle with sufferings, [33] sometimes being publicly exposed to reproach and affliction, and sometimes being partners with those so treated. [34] For you had compassion on those in prison, and you joyfully accepted the plundering of your property, since you knew that you yourselves had a better possession and an abiding one. [35] Therefore do not throw away your confidence, which has a great reward. [36] For you have need of endurance, so that when you have done the will of God you may receive what is promised. [37] For,

"Yet a little while,
    and the coming one will come and will not delay;
[38] but my righteous one shall live by faith,
    and if he shrinks back,
my soul has no pleasure in him."
[39] But we are not of those who shrink back and are destroyed, but of those who have faith and preserve their souls.

## HEBREWS 11

### BY FAITH

Now faith is the assurance of things hoped for, the conviction of things not seen. [2]For by it the people of old received their commendation. [3]By faith we understand that the universe was created by the word of God, so that what is seen was not made out of things that are visible.

[4]By faith Abel offered to God a more acceptable sacrifice than Cain, through which he was commended as righteous, God commending him by accepting his gifts. And through his faith, though he died, he still speaks. [5]By faith Enoch was taken up so that he should not see death, and he was not found, because God had taken him. Now before he was taken he was commended as having pleased God. [6]And without faith it is impossible to please him, for whoever would draw near to God must believe that he exists and that he rewards those who seek him. [7]By faith Noah, being warned by God concerning events as yet unseen, in reverent fear constructed an ark for the saving of his household. By this he condemned the world and became an heir of the righteousness that comes by faith.

[8]By faith Abraham obeyed when he was called to go out to a place that he was to receive as an inheritance. And he went out, not knowing where he was going. [9]By faith he went to live in the land of promise, as in a foreign land, living in tents with Isaac and Jacob, heirs with him of the same promise. [10]For he was looking forward to the city that has foundations, whose designer and builder is God. [11]By faith Sarah herself received power to conceive, even when she was past the age, since she considered him faithful who had promised. [12]Therefore from one man, and him as good as dead, were born descendants as many as the stars of heaven and as many as the innumerable grains of sand by the seashore.

[13]These all died in faith, not having received the things promised, but having seen them and greeted them from afar, and having acknowledged that they were strangers and exiles on the earth. [14]For people who speak

thus make it clear that they are seeking a homeland. [15]If they had been thinking of that land from which they had gone out, they would have had opportunity to return. [16]But as it is, they desire a better country, that is, a heavenly one. Therefore God is not ashamed to be called their God, for he has prepared for them a city.

[17]By faith Abraham, when he was tested, offered up Isaac, and he who had received the promises was in the act of offering up his only son, [18]of whom it was said, "Through Isaac shall your offspring be named." [19]He considered that God was able even to raise him from the dead, from which, figuratively speaking, he did receive him back. [20]By faith Isaac invoked future blessings on Jacob and Esau. [21]By faith Jacob, when dying, blessed each of the sons of Joseph, bowing in worship over the head of his staff. [22]By faith Joseph, at the end of his life, made mention of the exodus of the Israelites and gave directions concerning his bones.

[23]By faith Moses, when he was born, was hidden for three months by his parents, because they saw that the child was beautiful, and they were not afraid of the king's edict. [24]By faith Moses, when he was grown up, refused to be called the son of Pharaoh's daughter, [25]choosing rather to be mistreated with the people of God than to enjoy the fleeting pleasures of sin. [26]He considered the reproach of Christ greater wealth than the treasures of Egypt, for he was looking to the reward. [27]By faith he left Egypt, not being afraid of the anger of the king, for he endured as seeing him who is invisible. [28]By faith he kept the Passover and sprinkled the blood, so that the Destroyer of the firstborn might not touch them.

[29]By faith the people crossed the Red Sea as on dry land, but the Egyptians, when they attempted to do the same, were drowned. [30]By faith the walls of Jericho fell down after they had been encircled for seven days. [31]By faith Rahab the prostitute did not perish with those who were disobedient, because she had given a friendly welcome to the spies.

[32]And what more shall I say? For time would fail me to tell of Gideon,

Barak, Samson, Jephthah, of David and Samuel and the prophets—[33]who through faith conquered kingdoms, enforced justice, obtained promises, stopped the mouths of lions, [34]quenched the power of fire, escaped the edge of the sword, were made strong out of weakness, became mighty in war, put foreign armies to flight. [35]Women received back their dead by resurrection. Some were tortured, refusing to accept release, so that they might rise again to a better life. [36]Others suffered mocking and flogging, and even chains and imprisonment. [37]They were stoned, they were sawn in two, they were killed with the sword. They went about in skins of sheep and goats, destitute, afflicted, mistreated—[38]of whom the world was not worthy—wandering about in deserts and mountains, and in dens and caves of the earth.

[39]And all these, though commended through their faith, did not receive what was promised, [40]since God had provided something better for us, that apart from us they should not be made perfect.

## HEBREWS 12

### JESUS, FOUNDER AND PERFECTER OF OUR FAITH

Therefore, since we are surrounded by so great a cloud of witnesses, let us also lay aside every weight, and sin which clings so closely, and let us run with endurance the race that is set before us, [2]looking to Jesus, the founder and perfecter of our faith, who for the joy that was set before him endured the cross, despising the shame, and is seated at the right hand of the throne of God.

### DO NOT GROW WEARY

[3]Consider him who endured from sinners such hostility against himself, so that you may not grow weary or fainthearted. [4]In your struggle against sin you have not yet resisted to the point of shedding your blood. [5]And have

you forgotten the exhortation that addresses you as sons?
"My son, do not regard lightly the discipline of the Lord,

nor be weary when reproved by him.

⁶For the Lord disciplines the one he loves,

and chastises every son whom he receives."

⁷It is for discipline that you have to endure. God is treating you as sons. For what son is there whom his father does not discipline? ⁸If you are left without discipline, in which all have participated, then you are illegitimate children and not sons. ⁹Besides this, we have had earthly fathers who disciplined us and we respected them. Shall we not much more be subject to the Father of spirits and live? ¹⁰For they disciplined us for a short time as it seemed best to them, but he disciplines us for our good, that we may share his holiness. ¹¹For the moment all discipline seems painful rather than pleasant, but later it yields the peaceful fruit of righteousness to those who have been trained by it.

¹²Therefore lift your drooping hands and strengthen your weak knees, ¹³and make straight paths for your feet, so that what is lame may not be put out of joint but rather be healed. ¹⁴Strive for peace with everyone, and for the holiness without which no one will see the Lord. ¹⁵See to it that no one fails to obtain the grace of God; that no "root of bitterness" springs up and causes trouble, and by it many become defiled; ¹⁶that no one is sexually immoral or unholy like Esau, who sold his birthright for a single meal. ¹⁷For you know that afterward, when he desired to inherit the blessing, he was rejected, for he found no chance to repent, though he sought it with tears.

## A KINGDOM THAT CANNOT BE SHAKEN

¹⁸For you have not come to what may be touched, a blazing fire and darkness and gloom and a tempest ¹⁹and the sound of a trumpet and a voice whose words made the hearers beg that no further messages be spoken to them. ²⁰For they could not endure the order that was given,

"If even a beast touches the mountain, it shall be stoned." [21]Indeed, so terrifying was the sight that Moses said, "I tremble with fear." [22]But you have come to Mount Zion and to the city of the living God, the heavenly Jerusalem, and to innumerable angels in festal gathering, [23]and to the assembly of the firstborn who are enrolled in heaven, and to God, the judge of all, and to the spirits of the righteous made perfect, [24]and to Jesus, the mediator of a new covenant, and to the sprinkled blood that speaks a better word than the blood of Abel.

[25]See that you do not refuse him who is speaking. For if they did not escape when they refused him who warned them on earth, much less will we escape if we reject him who warns from heaven. [26]At that time his voice shook the earth, but now he has promised, "Yet once more I will shake not only the earth but also the heavens." [27]This phrase, "Yet once more," indicates the removal of things that are shaken—that is, things that have been made—in order that the things that cannot be shaken may remain. [28]Therefore let us be grateful for receiving a kingdom that cannot be shaken, and thus let us offer to God acceptable worship, with reverence and awe, [29]for our God is a consuming fire.

## HEBREWS 13

### SACRIFICES PLEASING TO GOD

Let brotherly love continue. [2]Do not neglect to show hospitality to strangers, for thereby some have entertained angels unawares. [3]Remember those who are in prison, as though in prison with them, and those who are mistreated, since you also are in the body. [4]Let marriage be held in honor among all, and let the marriage bed be undefiled, for God will judge the sexually immoral and adulterous. [5]Keep your life free from love of money, and be content with what you have, for he has said, "I will never leave you nor forsake you." [6]So we can confidently say,

"The Lord is my helper;

    I will not fear;

what can man do to me?"

[7] Remember your leaders, those who spoke to you the word of God. Consider the outcome of their way of life, and imitate their faith. [8] Jesus Christ is the same yesterday and today and forever. [9] Do not be led away by diverse and strange teachings, for it is good for the heart to be strengthened by grace, not by foods, which have not benefited those devoted to them. [10] We have an altar from which those who serve the tent have no right to eat. [11] For the bodies of those animals whose blood is brought into the holy places by the high priest as a sacrifice for sin are burned outside the camp. [12] So Jesus also suffered outside the gate in order to sanctify the people through his own blood. [13] Therefore let us go to him outside the camp and bear the reproach he endured. [14] For here we have no lasting city, but we seek the city that is to come. [15] Through him then let us continually offer up a sacrifice of praise to God, that is, the fruit of lips that acknowledge his name. [16] Do not neglect to do good and to share what you have, for such sacrifices are pleasing to God.

[17] Obey your leaders and submit to them, for they are keeping watch over your souls, as those who will have to give an account. Let them do this with joy and not with groaning, for that would be of no advantage to you. [18] Pray for us, for we are sure that we have a clear conscience, desiring to act honorably in all things. [19] I urge you the more earnestly to do this in order that I may be restored to you the sooner.

### BENEDICTION

[20] Now may the God of peace who brought again from the dead our Lord Jesus, the great shepherd of the sheep, by the blood of the eternal covenant, [21] equip you with everything good that you may do his will,

working in us that which is pleasing in his sight, through Jesus Christ, to whom be glory forever and ever. Amen.

## FINAL GREETINGS

[22]I appeal to you, brothers, bear with my word of exhortation, for I have written to you briefly. [23]You should know that our brother Timothy has been released, with whom I shall see you if he comes soon. [24]Greet all your leaders and all the saints. Those who come from Italy send you greetings. [25]Grace be with all of you.

## APPENDIX | THE ATTRIBUTES OF GOD

**Attentive:** God hears and responds to the needs of His children.

**Compassionate:** God cares for His children and acts on their behalf.

**Creator:** God made everything. He is uncreated.

**Deliverer:** God rescues and saves His children.

**Eternal:** God is not limited by time; He exists outside of time.

**Faithful:** God always keeps His promises.

**Generous:** God gives what is best and beyond what is deserved.

**Glorious:** God displays His greatness and worth.

**Good:** God is what is best and gives what is best. He is incapable of doing harm.

**Holy:** God is perfect, pure, and without sin.

**Immutable/Unchanging:** God never changes. He is the same yesterday, today, and tomorrow.

**Incomprehensible:** God is beyond our understanding. We can comprehend Him in part but not in whole.

**Infinite:** God has no limits in His person or on His power.

**Jealous:** God will not share His glory with another. All glory rightfully belongs to Him.

**Just:** God is fair in all His actions and judgments. He cannot over-punish or under-punish.

**Loving:** God feels and displays infinite, unconditional affection toward His children. His love for them does not depend on their worth, response, or merit.

**Merciful:** God does not give His children the punishment they deserve.

**Omnipotent/Almighty:** God holds all power. Nothing is too hard for God. What He wills He can accomplish.

**Omnipresent:** God is fully present everywhere.

**Omniscient:** God knows everything, past, present, and future—all potential and real outcomes, all things micro and macro.

Patient/Long-suffering: God is untiring and bears with His children.

Provider: God meets the needs of His children.

Refuge: God is a place of safety and protection for His children.

Righteous: God is always good and right.

Self-existent: God depends on nothing and no one to give Him life or existence.

Self-sufficient: God is not vulnerable. He has no needs.

Sovereign: God does everything according to His plan and pleasure. He controls all things.

Transcendent: God is not like humans. He is infinitely higher in being and action.

Truthful: Whatever God speaks or does is truth and reality.

Wise: God knows what is best and acts accordingly. He cannot choose wrongly.

Worthy: God deserves all glory and honor and praise

Wrathful: God hates all unrighteousness..

# Other Studies
## by Jen Wilkin

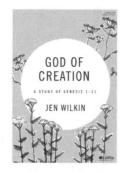

### GOD OF CREATION
10 Sessions

Dive into the first 11 chapters of Genesis to revisit familiar stories and discover deeper meanings in the text.

LifeWay.com/GodOfCreation

### GOD OF COVENANT
10 Sessions

Walk alongside the fathers of our faith in Genesis 12–50—Abraham, Isaac, Jacob, and Joseph—to discern Jesus in the stories of His people.

LifeWay.com/GodOfCovenant

### 1 PETER: A LIVING HOPE IN CHRIST
9 Sessions

Study the Book of 1 Peter to look beyond your current circumstances to a future inheritance through Christ.

LifeWay.com/1PeterStudy

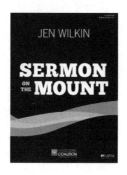

### SERMON ON THE MOUNT
9 Sessions

Study Jesus' Sermon on the Mount verse by verse to learn what it means to be a citizen of the kingdom of heaven.

LifeWay.com/
SermonOnTheMount

**LifeWay.com/JenWilkin**
800.458.2772

LifeWay | **Women**